ATLAS OF RECORD-BREAKING ADVENTURES

WIDE EYED EDITIONS

North America

Africa

Central America

South America

WORLD MAP

Antarctica

Europe

Asia

Middle
East

Australasia
& Oceania

N

W   E

S

CONTENTS

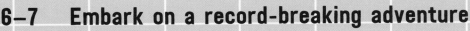

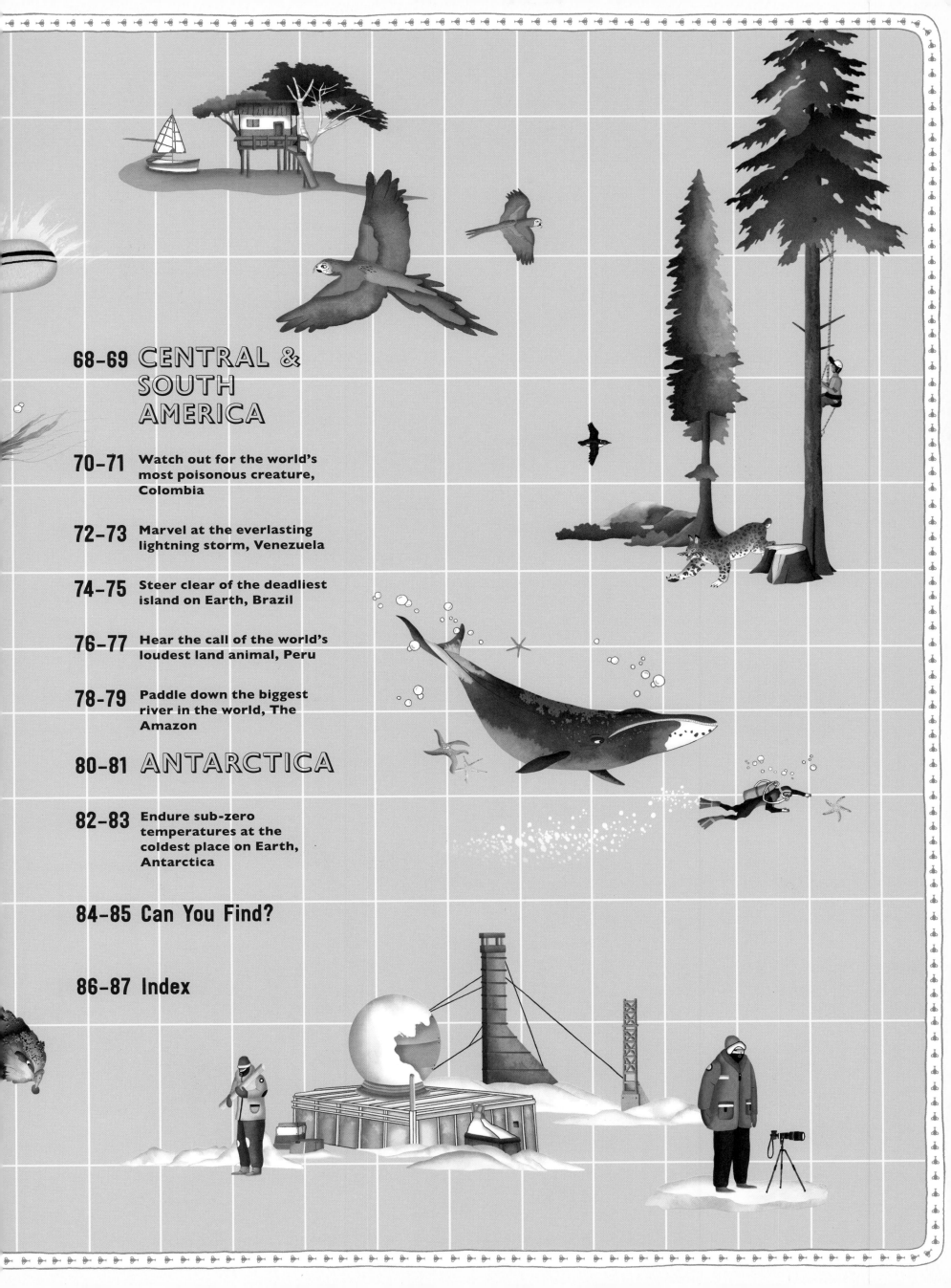

Cheetah

Danakil Desert

Victoria Falls

Marathon Des Sables

Mountain gorillas

Cuvier's beaked whale

Catacombs of Paris

Greenland shark

Mount Stromboli

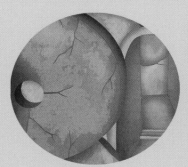

Derinkuyu Underground City

Trans-Siberian Railway

Mongol Derby

Yarlung Tsangpo

Hang Son Doong

Titan arum

Black marlin

Termites

Waitomo Caves

Kakapo

Lake Superior

BREAKING ADVENTURE

Peregrine falcon

Prairie dogs

Cave of Swallows

Lake Maracaibo

Howler monkeys

The Amazon

Vostok research station

The world is full of record-breaking wonders. This book will take you on a trip around the globe to discover some of our planet's most extreme animals, incredible places, amazing plants, and astonishing human feats.

Meet the animal record-breakers, from the fastest creatures on Earth to the largest, oldest, noisiest, and most poisonous beasts. Explore some natural marvels, including the world's biggest waterfall, the longest-erupting volcano, and the most enormous cave. You'll come face to face with the planet's most bizarre plants, from the smelliest flower to the most deadly tree. And you'll discover a host of human-made wonders, such as the deepest underground city, the longest railway, and even the largest collection of skeletons on Earth. Prepare to embark on an eye-opening world tour!

Redwoods

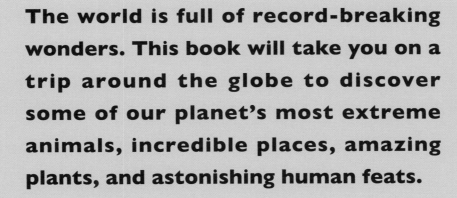

Manchineel tree

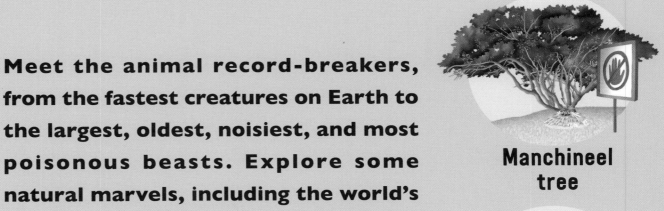

Golden poison frog

Snake Island

AFRICA

With 54 nations, Africa has the most countries of any continent on Earth. You'll have heard about Africa's record-breaking wildlife, from its huge elephants to its tall giraffes and super-speedy cheetahs. But you'll also find many other record-breakers, from natural marvels such as the world's biggest waterfall to lesser-known wonders like the largest mud building and the most enormous pink lake.

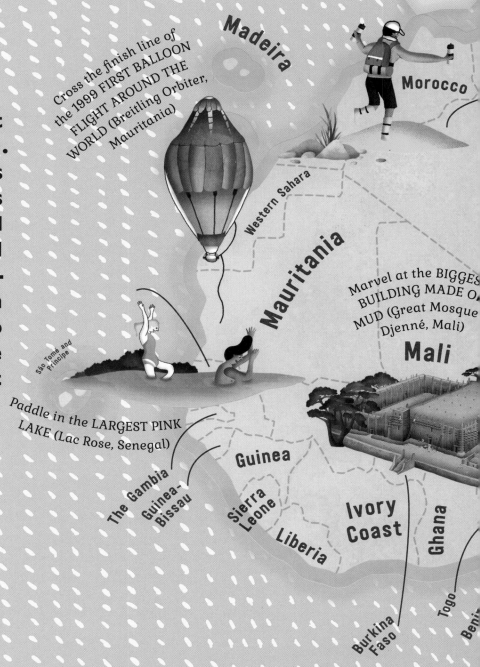

Cross the finish line of the 1999 FIRST BALLOON FLIGHT AROUND THE WORLD (Breitling Orbiter, Mauritania)

Madeira

Morocco

Western Sahara

Mauritania

Marvel at the BIGGES... BUILDING MADE O... MUD (Great Mosque ... Djenné, Mali)

Mali

São Tomé and Príncipe

Paddle in the LARGEST PINK LAKE (Lac Rose, Senegal)

The Gambia

Guinea-Bissau

Guinea

Sierra Leone

Liberia

Ivory Coast

Ghana

Togo

Benin

Burkina Faso

North Atlantic Ocean

Ascension Island

St Helena

South Atlantic Ocean

Tunisia

See the world's TALLEST PYRAMID (Pyramid of Khufu, Giza, Egypt)

Survive the MOST EXTREME HUMAN ENDURANCE RUN (Marathon Des Sables, Morocco)

Libya

Egypt

The Middle East

Algeria

Feel the heat in the BIGGEST HOT DESERT (The Sahara, North Africa)

Brave the HOTTEST PLACE On Earth (Danakil Desert, Ethiopia)

Niger

Sudan

Eritrea

Arabian Sea

Chad

South Sudan

Nigeria

Central African Republic

Meet the world's LARGEST PRIMATE (Gorilla, Rwanda)

Ethiopia

Somalia

Cameroon

Congo

Uganda

Kenya

Equatorial Guinea

Gabon

Rwanda

Burundi

Look out for the LARGEST FRESHWATER MAMMAL (Hippo, Tanzania)

Seychelles

Hold on tight along the WORLD'S DEEPEST RIVER (Congo River)

Democratic Republic of the Congo

Tanzania

Discover the world's LARGEST COBWEBS (Darwin's Bark Spider, Madagascar)

Don't upset the MOST SUCCESSFUL PREDATOR (African Hunting Dog, Zimbabwe)

Comoros

Cool off at the world's BIGGEST WATERFALL (Victoria Falls, Zambia)

Angola

Mayotte

Zambia

Malawi

Madagascar

Mauritius

Spot one of the BIGGEST BIRDS' NESTS (Social Weaver Birds, Namibia)

Zimbabwe

Race against the FASTEST LAND ANIMAL (Cheetah, Botswana)

Namibia

Botswana

Mozambique

Swim with the MOST ENORMOUS FISH (Whale Shark, Mozambique)

Reunion

Indian Ocean

Enter the world's LARGEST CYCLING RACE (Cape Town Cycle Tour, South Africa)

Swaziland

Cross the WIDEST METEORITE CRATER (Vredefort Crater, South Africa)

South Africa

Climb the OLDEST MOUNTAIN RANGE (Makhonjwa Mountains, Swaziland)

FASTEST LAND ANIMAL, BOTSWANA

All is quiet on the savanna. Under the glare of the hot sun, antelopes and zebras cool off by the waterhole, their tails gently flicking the flies away. But suddenly, the creatures are startled by a flash of movement. A hungry cheetah bounds from her hiding place in the long grass, scattering a herd of impalas. The cheetah has a young impala in her sights, and the pair streak across the landscape, leaving clouds of dust in their wake.

The impala is fast, but the cheetah is faster. In fact, the cheetah is the fastest land animal on the planet, able to reach a top speed of over 60 miles per hour: more than twice as fast as the quickest human sprinter. When a cheetah is running at full pelt, it can cover 23 feet (or the length of an elephant) in a single stride. But the cheetah is not the only record breaker on the African savanna: many creatures here have their own claims to fame.

Weighing up to 330 pounds, the same as a panda, the ostrich is the world's heaviest bird. It's also the fastest creature on two legs... and it lays the largest eggs!

A cheetah cub has a mane of fur on its back, which makes it look like an aggressive honey badger. This helps ward off attackers.

A cheetah can accelerate from zero to 55 miles per hour in just three seconds—faster than the average car.

While sprinting, a cheetah is airborne (with all four paws off the ground) for more than half of the time.

Unlike other cats, the cheetah can't retract its claws. Instead, they grip the ground like running spikes while the cheetah is sprinting, keeping it steady.

Giraffes are the tallest land animals on Earth, with males reaching a lofty 19 feet. And their black tongues are huge as well, at lengths of up to 20 inches.

The African elephant is the world's heaviest land animal, weighing in at six tons, which is about the same as three family cars.

Okovango Delta

BOTSWANA

At over three feet long, an elephant's ears are the largest on the planet. Also, with a six-foot trunk, it scoops the prize for the longest nose of any animal.

The cheetah's long tail whips from side to side as it zig-zags through the grass in pursuit of prey. This helps counterbalance the cat, so it doesn't topple over.

Long tail, for balance and to help it turn in the air

Dark lines around eyes help reduce glare from the sun

Stride length: 23 feet

Sleek, streamlined body

Long, powerful legs

The hot springs are surrounded by miles of salt flats: plains of land covered in salt crystals, which gleam white under the baking sun.

The local Afar people mine salt from this dry landscape, and carry it across the desert using camels.

This area is home to the saltiest lake in the world. The Gaet'ale Pond is 43.3% salt: that's 12 times as salty as the ocean.

These crusty splodges of bright yellow, orange, and green are made from minerals, such as sulfur and iron, that are brought to the surface by bubbling spring water.

There are several active volcanoes in the region. One, called Erta Ale, has two bubbling lava lakes at its summit.

12

Scientists who study these hot springs sometimes wear gas masks to protect them from the toxic fumes.

Danakil Desert

ETHIOPIA

Few plants or animals can survive among the boiling, acidic pools. However, scientists have discovered bacteria living here in what must be one of the most extreme environments on Earth.

Working out the hottest place is tricky. Another way of measuring it is to look at the highest single temperature ever recorded. One day in 2005, the ground in the Lut Desert, Iran, reached a whopping 159°F: hot enough to fry an egg!

The Danakil Desert is not only one of the hottest places on Earth, it is one of the driest too, with almost no rainfall.

BRAVE THE

HOTTEST PLACE ON EARTH, ETHIOPIA

Nicknamed "Hell on Earth" and a "land of death," the Danakil Desert in north-east Ethiopia is not everyone's top choice for a holiday destination. The blistering sunshine and lack of rain make this scorching desert an uncomfortable spot to spend time in. It's the hottest place on Earth if you look at the average weather all year round. Here, temperatures normally hover around 93.9°F, but can soar to 131°F in summer.

Visiting Danakil is like arriving on another planet. It lies in an area of volcanic activity, so the landscape is strewn with bubbling lava lakes and neon rock formations. There are thermal springs here, but you wouldn't want to bathe in them: these bright-green pools are not only filled with acid, but are also scalding hot. Remember to pack your sunscreen, a hat, and gallons of water... you're going to need them.

The dramatic spray from the falls rises 1,640 feet into the air and often creates rainbows.

The thundering roar from these plunging waters can be heard from over a mile away.

ZAMBIA

ZIMBABWE

Victoria Falls

The Victoria Falls were formed hundreds of thousands of years ago by the flow of the Zambezi River slicing into the rocky plateau over which it runs.

COOL OFF AT THE WORLD'S
BIGGEST WATERFALL, ZAMBIA

With a span of 5,580 feet and a drop of more than 350 feet, the Victoria Falls is the most enormous waterfall in the world. This spectacular curtain of water, whose spray can be seen from 12 miles away, is known as Mosi-oa-Tunya by the locals, which means "the smoke that thunders." These falls bridge two countries: the border between Zimbabwe and Zambia lies in the middle.

At the top of this natural wonder, just before the water plummets into the gaping canyon below, is the Devil's Swimming Pool. Believe it or not, when the water level is just right, brave swimmers can go for a dip here! Although it looks terrifying, there is a natural barrier of rock just below the surface, which stops people from being washed over the edge. The view from the brink into the gorge beneath is dizzying.

In 2014, two daredevils crossed the Victoria Falls on a 1.2-inch-wide slackline!

If you don't have a head for heights, don't look down!

You can only swim in the Devil's Pool with experienced guides, during the dry season (usually from September to December) when the water level isn't too high.

This waterfall breaks the record for being the world's largest sheet of falling water. Angel Falls in Venezuela is the world's highest waterfall, at 3,211 feet.

The drop from the top of the falls is taller than London's Big Ben clock tower, and spans over 17 soccer fields in width.

In the rainy season, when the flow is strongest, almost 720,000 gallons—or an Olympic swimming pool of water—surges over the edge of the falls every two seconds!

Height: 354 feet

Width: 5,580 feet

Desert hat to protect against sun

Goggles in case of sandstorms

Neckerchief can be pulled over mouth to stop runners breathing in sand

Bottle holders

Gaiters to stop sand getting inside shoes

The Sahara Desert, which stretches across North Africa, is the largest hot desert in the world.

Runners are advised to wear extra-large running shoes, because people's feet swell up in the heat.

The youngest competitor ever to take part was 16... the oldest was 78.

The marathon route varies from year to year. The longest stage, which is usually about 55 miles, can involve running through the night.

Runners have to carry everything they need excluding water, which is handed out along the route. Packs must contain emergency equipment, including an anti-venom pump for snakebites.

The support crew and kit are made up of 52 doctors, seven planes, six satellite phones, four quad bikes, two helicopters, and four camels.

MOROCCO

Marathon Des Sables

The race is so exhausting that many participants walk most of the way, instead of running.

The most successful competitor ever is the Moroccan runner Lahcen Ahansal, who has won this event a record ten times.

In 1994, after a sandstorm along the route, an Italian athlete named Mauro Prosperi became lost in the desert for ten days. He survived by drinking cacti juice and the blood from a bat!

In 2019 a dog named Diggedy joined runners. He finished the race, covering more than 99 miles. He even battled through a sandstorm and was awarded a medal.

SURVIVE THE
MOST EXTREME HUMAN ENDURANCE RUN, MOROCCO

Imagine running an ultra-marathon, covering a total of 155 miles—or the equivalent of six standard marathons—in just six days. Now imagine doing it while carrying a heavy backpack, containing your food, clothes, a sleeping bag, and cooking equipment. Now, imagine enduring all this in the Sahara Desert, in blazing 121°F heat! This is the challenge faced by competitors in the Marathon Des Sables, or Marathon of the Sands. This gruelling event is said to be the toughest race on Earth.

The Marathon Des Sables takes place in the southern Moroccan desert every year. The very first race was run in 1986, with just 23 competitors. These days, there are more than 1,000 participants, from all over the world. These tough athletes may have to face sandstorms, excruciating blisters, heatstroke, dehydration, venomous snakes, and scorpions. This event pushes people to their limits—it takes huge amounts of determination and strength, both physical and mental, to reach the finish line

Mountain gorilla habitat

UGANDA

DRC

RWANDA

Mountain gorillas spend a third of every day eating. They forage for roots, shoots, tree bark, and pulp.

Gorillas produce huge amounts of gas while digesting all this veg... listen out for their enormous farts!

The mountain gorilla is the world's largest and heaviest primate. Silverbacks can stand five and a half feet tall and weigh 440 pounds—about the same as 30 bowling balls.

Tiny babies cling to their mother's fur, and will ride on her back until they are two or three years old.

Yucky fact: gorillas sometimes eat their own dung. Scientists think this may help them take in nutrients that their bodies didn't absorb first time around.

Adult male has a saddle of silver hair

Mountain gorillas have thicker hair than other gorillas, to keep them warm in their high-altitude habitats

Thanks to the efforts of conservationists, mountain gorilla numbers are slowly creeping up. In 2006 there were fewer than 350 left in the wild. Today, there are thought to be over 1,000.

Gorillas are very closely related to humans: we share 98% of the same DNA.

These incredible creatures are under threat from habitat loss, poaching, and diseases such as the common cold, which can be passed on by humans.

MEET THE WORLD'S
LARGEST PRIMATE, RWANDA

In Rwanda's Virunga Mountains, thickly forested volcanoes rise up into the clouds. Here live some of the world's largest and rarest primates: mountain gorillas. These gentle giants are peaceful creatures who spend their days grazing, grooming, playing, and resting. They live in troops of about 10 to 20, each led by one large, dominant male. This huge, powerful creature has a saddle of silver hair across his back, earning him the name "silverback."

While the adult gorillas rest among the trees after a morning of feeding, the youngsters scamper around them. They swing, hang, tumble, and wrestle. The teenage males jostle for prime position, showing off their strength. One of them stands upright on his hind legs, beating his chest and hooting loudly. It's an impressive display, but not impressive enough to threaten the silverback. He rests easy in the knowledge that he is in charge, at least for the time being.

Greenland

Pay your respects to the WORLD'S OLDEST VERTEBRATE (Greenland Shark, Greenland)

Snap a selfie outside the world's LARGEST SEED VAULT (Svalbard, Norway)

↑ Svalbard

Iceland

Watch out for the world's LARGEST JELLYFISH (Lion's Mane Jellyfish, North Atlantic)

Faroe Islands

Shetland Islands

EUROPE

Europe is overflowing with human-made wonders, including the oldest hedge maze, the tallest church, and the longest pedestrian bridge in the world. Here, you'll also come across some of the more bizarre record-breakers, including the planet's biggest collection of skeletons, the sheep with the most horns, and the world's heaviest building!

Butt up against the SHEEP WITH THE MOST HORNS (Four-Horned Jacob Sheep, UK)

Size up the 180-foot LONGEST ANIMAL (Bootlace Worm, North Sea)

Denmark

Take the train through the LONGEST UNDERSEA TUNNEL (Channel Tunnel, UK/France)

United Kingdom

Ireland

Get lost in the world's OLDEST HEDGE MAZE (Hampton Court, UK)

Netherlands

Belgium

Admire the view from the TALLEST CHURCH (Ulm Minster, Germany)

Look around the world's LARGEST MUSEUM (The Louvre, Paris, France)

Marvel at the world's LARGEST COLLECTION OF HUMAN BONES (Catacombs, France)

France

Switzerland

Atlantic Ocean

Hold your breath with NATURE'S BEST AIR-BREATHING DIVER (Cuvier's Beaked Whale, The Azores)

Spain

Andorra

Cross the LONGEST PEDESTRIAN BRIDGE (Zermatt, Switzerland)

Corsica

The Azores

Test the strength of the STRONGEST ANIMAL FOR ITS SIZE (Taurus dung beetle, Spain)

Surf the beach of the 78-foot LARGEST WAVE EVER SURFED (Nazaré, Portugal)

Portugal

Balearic Islands

Sardinia

Mediterranean Sea

Africa

Norway

Sweden

Finland

Barents Sea

White Sea

Baltic Sea

Russia

Drive along the 15.5-mile LONGEST ROAD TUNNEL (Laerdal Tunnel, Norway)

Gotland

Estonia

Latvia

Check out the birthplace of Yuri Gargarin, the FIRST PERSON IN SPACE (Klushino, Russia)

Lithuania

Kaliningrad

Belarus

Poland

Czech Republic

Feel the freeze in the BIGGEST ICE CAVE (Austria)

Ukraine

Slovakia

Moldova

Romania

Austria

Hungary

Slovenia

Take a tour of the SMALLEST COUNTRY IN THE WORLD (Vatican City)

Croatia

Bosnia and Herzegovina

Serbia

See the world's HEAVIEST BUILDING (Palace of the Parliament, Bucharest, Romania)

Black Sea

Asia

Montenegro

Kosovo

North Macedonia

Bulgaria

Turkey

Italy

Albania

Greece

Turkey

Visit the world's LONGEST-ERUPTING VOLCANO (Stromboli, Italy)

Malta

21

HOLD YOUR BREATH WITH NATURE'S
BEST AIR-BREATHING DIVER, THE AZORES

Prepare to meet the world champion of deep-sea diving. Cuvier's beaked whale is a rarely-seen animal that lives far out at sea, in the Atlantic, Pacific, and Indian oceans. In 2013 scientists attached electronic tags to eight of these whales, and recorded their dives. They were amazed to discover that this incredible creature can plunge as deep as 9,816 feet, which is nearly 10 times the height of the Eiffel Tower! This impressive feat makes Cuvier's beaked whale the deepest-diving mammal on the planet.

And that's not all... this whale also claims the record for the longest dive by a mammal ever recorded, lasting a whopping two hours, 17 minutes and 30 seconds. Imagine trying to hold your breath for that long! For comparison, in 2014 a champion free-diver named Branko Petrovic broke the human record by holding his breath underwater for 11 minutes, 54 seconds. Good thing he didn't have to compete against a Cuvier's whale!

The cookie-cutter shark is a small, deep-diving shark. It gets its name because it gouges round plugs of flesh from its prey. Many Cuvier's whales have circular scars caused by cookie-cutter bites!

Cuvier's whale is named after the French naturalist Georges Cuvier, who described the species in 1823, based on a fragment of skull discovered on a beach...

Cuvier thought the skull was an ancient fossil from an extinct whale. After his death another zoologist found the species to be alive and well!

Another ocean record-breaker is the blue whale. This mighty beast measures up to 98 feet long, similar to a Boeing 737 aircraft. Its heart is the size of a small car, and its tongue weighs as much as an African elephant.

Cuvier's whales sometimes swallow plastic bags, mistaking them for squid. One dead whale was found with 88 pounds of plastic clogging up its stomach.

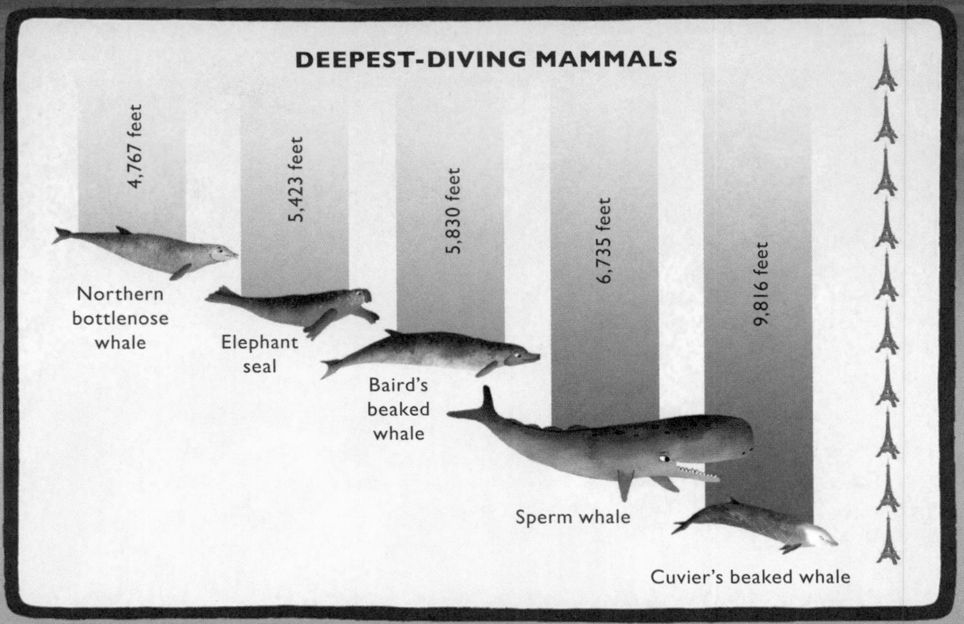

DEEPEST-DIVING MAMMALS

4,767 feet
Northern bottlenose whale

5,423 feet
Elephant seal

5,830 feet
Baird's beaked whale

6,735 feet
Sperm whale

9,816 feet
Cuvier's beaked whale

Before taking the plunge, the whale breathes out nearly all of the air from its lungs. This reduces its buoyancy, making it easier to plummet downwards.

The deeper you go, the greater the pressure of water pushing down from above. At 0.6 miles deep, a whale's body is under 100 times more pressure than it is at the surface.

If you were to dive this far down, the pressure would crush you—so how does the whale cope? It's able to fold down its rib cage and collapse its lungs, so they don't get damaged.

As it dives, the whale's heart-rate slows down, to help it conserve oxygen. It also stores oxygen in its blood and muscles—just like having a built-in scuba-tank.

Why do Cuvier's whales dive to such depths? It's because they're on the hunt for food, particularly squid.

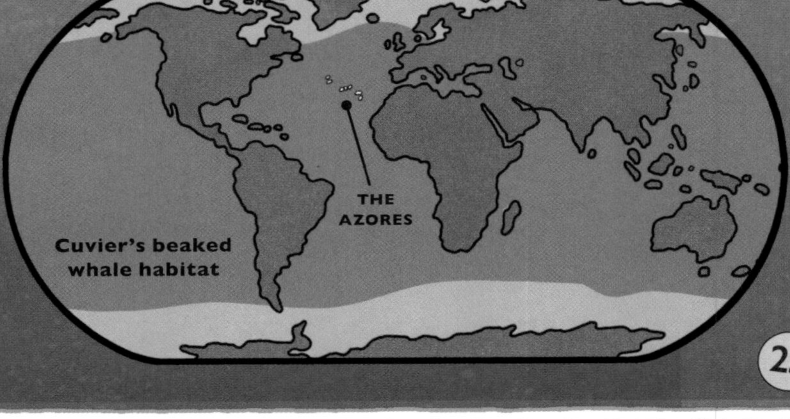

THE AZORES

Cuvier's beaked whale habitat

The bones are arranged in various shapes and patterns.

The bones were moved to the Catacombs during the 1780s. Bone carts trundled through the streets at night, draped in black cloths, accompanied by chanting priests with flaming torches.

The biggest cemetery that was emptied was Les Innocents. During a plague in the 15th century, 50,000 bodies were buried here in just one month.

An 'ossuary' is the name for a resting place for the bones of the dead.

In the Middle Ages it was quite common for people to dig up bones and store them in ossuaries, to free up space in graveyards.

MARVEL AT THE WORLD'S
LARGEST COLLECTION OF HUMAN BONES, FRANCE

"Halt! This is the empire of death." So reads the eerie inscription hanging over the entrance to the Catacombs of Paris. Beneath the city streets lies a maze of secrets. There are more than 186 miles of underground passageways, which were once limestone quarries, providing the stone with which the city was built. Most of these dangerous tunnels are off-limits to the public, but a tiny section is open for visitors. In these dimly lit chambers, the walls are lined with bones, stacked from floor to ceiling. This is thought to be the world's largest collection of human bones, containing the remains of six million people.

In the late 18th century the citizens of Paris had a problem. The cemeteries were full to bursting, packed with the bodies of thousands of plague victims, along with the rest of the city's dead. The overcrowded graveyards were causing a foul stench and spreading disease. In 1780, after months of heavy rain, the underground wall between a restaurant and a cemetery collapsed, spilling bodies into the restaurant basement. The citizens needed a better place to house their dead. The answer was to empty the cemeteries, transporting all the bones into the city's underground mines. Today, you can take a tour of the Catacombs to visit the final resting place of these ancient Parisians.

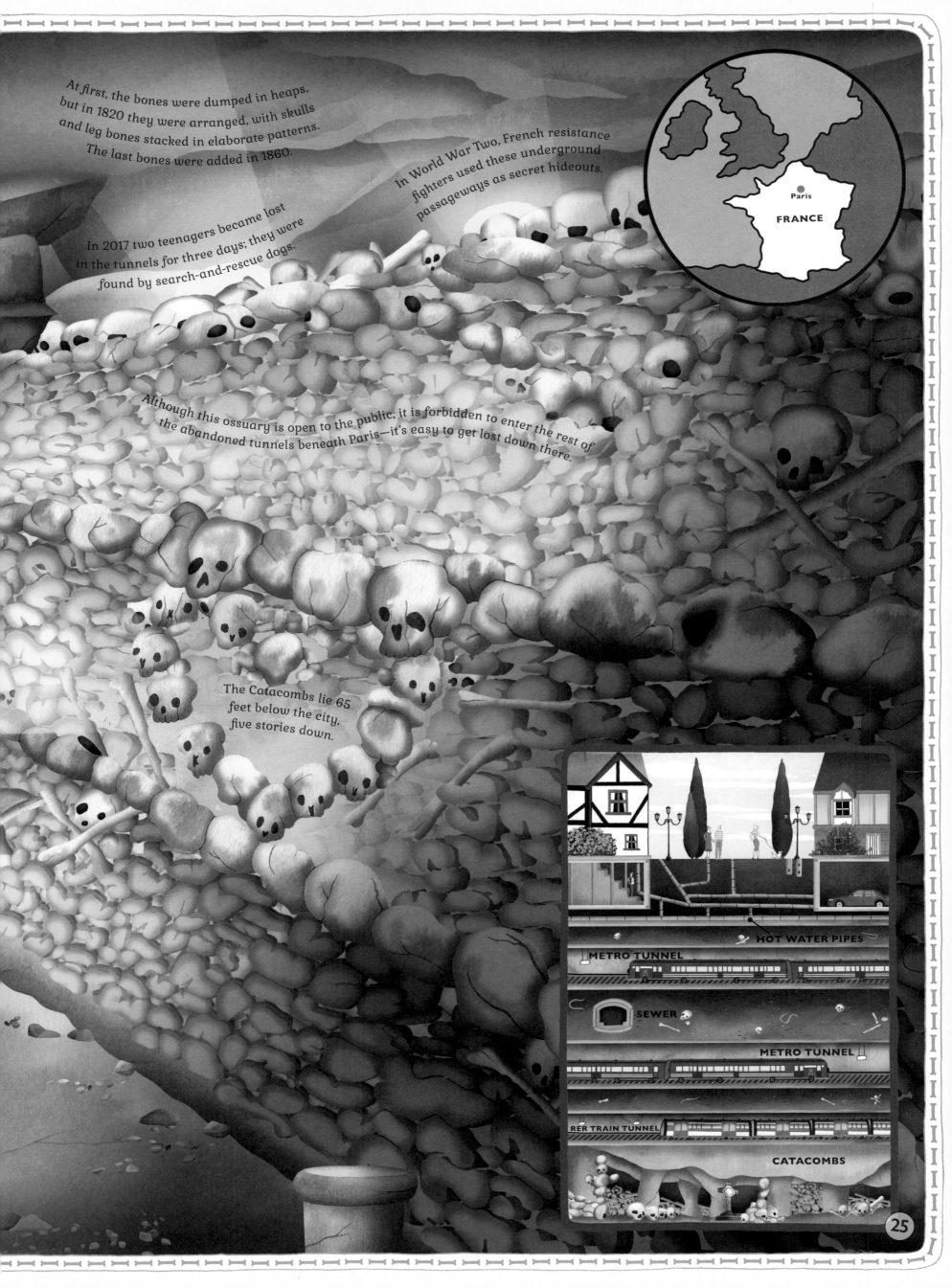

At first, the bones were dumped in heaps, but in 1820 they were arranged, with skulls and leg bones stacked in elaborate patterns. The last bones were added in 1860.

In World War Two, French resistance fighters used these underground passageways as secret hideouts.

In 2017 two teenagers became lost in the tunnels for three days; they were found by search-and-rescue dogs.

Although this ossuary is open to the public, it is forbidden to enter the rest of the abandoned tunnels beneath Paris—it's easy to get lost down there.

The Catacombs lie 65 feet below the city, five stories down.

FRANCE

Paris

HOT WATER PIPES

METRO TUNNEL

SEWER

METRO TUNNEL

RER TRAIN TUNNEL

CATACOMBS

PAY YOUR RESPECTS TO THE WORLD'S
OLDEST VERTEBRATE, GREENLAND

In the year 1616, the playwright William Shakespeare died and the astronomer Galileo was still trying to convince people that the Earth went round the Sun. Scientists think that around this time, more than 400 years ago, several sharks were born that would survive for centuries to come. They would live through the rise and fall of empires, outlasting revolutions and world wars. The Greenland shark, so the experts say, is the world's longest-living vertebrate (animal with a backbone).

In 2016, scientists used carbon dating to calculate the age of a group of Greenland sharks that had become tangled up in fishing nets. They worked out that the oldest shark, a female, was at least 272, and was perhaps as old as 512! She was likely to be about 400 years old. It's incredible that these sharks survive for so long, considering the dangers of a life at sea, including fishing trawlers, predators, and disease. It's possible that the cold water where they live switches on anti-aging genes in their bodies, helping the sharks fight off infections.

Greenland sharks live a long time but they are late bloomers. They don't settle down and have pups until they are about 150 years old!

The Greenland shark is a mysterious creature. It spends most of its time in the chilly depths of the Arctic and North Atlantic oceans, so it is tricky to study.

So, how do scientists work out the age of a sea creature? In some species of shark, they can count the rings inside the bones, like you would do with the rings of a tree...

...But Greenland sharks don't have hard bones, so the scientists needed a different tactic. To estimate the sharks' ages, they measured the types of carbon found in the lenses of their eyes.

Good sense of smell

Bad eyesight: many have parasites in their eyes, making them blind

Stomach may contain scavenged pieces of food, including the remains of reindeer and polar bears!

These sharks grow very slowly, at a rate of just 0.4 inches per year. They can eventually reach 23 feet.

These deep-ocean dwellers are very slow-moving. They swim at a sluggish pace of three feet every three seconds.

Which creature has the shortest life span? Some types of female mayfly live for less than five minutes—just enough time to mate and lay their eggs.

GREENLAND

Greenland shark habitat

The oldest human ever to have lived was Jeanne Louise Calment, from France. She was born in 1875 and died in 1997, reaching the ripe old age of 122.

The second-longest-living vertebrate is the bowhead whale. One bowhead, caught in 2007, was thought to be 211 years old. It had a 19th century whaling harpoon stuck in its neck.

Smashing all records, the oldest invertebrate (creature without a backbone) was a clam found off the coast of Iceland in 2006. Researchers counted the bands on its shell to work out its age... 507 years old!

Although they are so slow, these large sharks don't have many predators, other than sperm whales.

Stromboli often fires out lava bombs. These are scorching lumps of magma that rocket skywards. They cool and turn into solid chunks before they hit the ground.

There are about 1,500 active volcanoes in the world, on land. Most are in the Ring of Fire: an area around the Pacific Ocean famous for its eruptions.

At any one time, there are roughly 20 volcanoes erupting on Earth.

At night, the bursting flares of lava give off a fiery glow. For this reason, Stromboli has been nicknamed the Lighthouse of the Mediterranean.

Mount Etna, on the Italian island of Sicily, is the highest volcano in Europe, at around 10,925 feet tall. It is one of the world's most active volcanoes.

VISIT THE WORLD'S
LONGEST-ERUPTING VOLCANO, ITALY

The ground beneath our feet may appear to be stable, but it is actually on the move. The Earth's crust is divided into large pieces, called plates, which slowly float around on a layer of thick, partly molten rock. Sometimes, the plates collide, and one is forced beneath another. This causes red-hot magma from inside the Earth to rise to the surface, exploding out of volcanoes as lava. Off the coast of Italy is a record-breaking volcano that has been erupting continuously for at least 2,700 years... Mount Stromboli.

Stromboli lies just north of Sicily, in the Mediterranean Sea. Even though this small island is home to a very active volcano, there are still a few hundred people who live here. These residents have become used to the constant growling, rumbling, and spluttering of their enormous neighbor. It's like living with a grumpy dragon! Mount Stromboli usually erupts several times an hour. Normally, these eruptions involve small explosions of gas and smoke, and glowing showers of lava. But sometimes, they can be huge, with columns of ash rising hundreds of feet into the air.

At the summit, there are several different craters and vents which spew out ash, smoke, and lava.

In July 2019 Stromboli had a large explosion that sparked several wildfires, sending a plume of ash over a mile into the air.

Which country has the most volcanoes? The USA has 173. Its west coast lies on the Pacific Ring of Fire.

Another famous Italian volcano is Mount Vesuvius. An enormous eruption in 79CE buried the Roman cities of Pompeii and Herculaneum under a blanket of ash, killing about 16,000 people.

When the volcano Krakatoa erupted in Indonesia in 1883, it produced the loudest noise in recorded history, so deafening it was heard 3,106 miles away!

INSIDE A VOLCANO

Crater

Main vent

Side vent

Magma Chamber

Take a trip on the world's LONGEST RAILWAY (Trans-Siberian Railway, Russia)

Russia

Saddle up for THE LONGEST HORSE RACE IN THE WORLD (Mongol Derby, Mongolia)

Europe

Explore the world's DEEPEST UNDERGROUND CITY (Derinkuyu, Turkey)

Visit the world's BIGGEST LANDLOCKED COUNTRY (Kazakhstan)

Walk the world's LONGEST WALL (Great Wall of China)

Mongolia

Turkey

Georgia

Armenia

Azerbaijan

Caspian Sea

Kazakhstan

Uzbekistan

Kyrgyzstan

China

Ride rapids on the world's HIGHEST RIVER (Yarlung Tsangpo, Tibet)

Lebanon
Palestine
Israel Jordan

Syria

Turkmenistan

Tajikistan

Iraq **Iran**

Zoom along the world's LONGEST ZIPLINE (Jebel Jais Flight, UAE)

Afghanistan

Climb the HIGHEST MOUNTAIN (Mount Everest, Nepal/China)

Don't look down on the world's HIGHEST BRIDGE (Duge Bridge, China)

Saudi Arabia

UAE

Clean the windows of the world's TALLEST BUILDING (Burj Khalifa, Dubai)

Oman

Yemen

Pakistan

Bhutan

Nepal

India

Burma [Myanmar]

Laos

Come face to face with the LONGEST VENOMOUS SNAKE (King Cobra, India)

Cross the WORLD'S ONLY DOUBLE-DECKER ROOT BRIDGE (Cherrapunji, India)

India

Thailand

Africa

Shelter beneath the LARGEST TREE CANOPY (Thimmamma Marrimanu Banyan Tree, India)

Camb

Indian Ocean

Sri Lanka

Maldives

Sniff out the world's STINKIEST PLANT (Corpse Flower, Indonesia)

Seychelles

Chagos Archipelago

ASIA & THE MIDDLE EAST

Asia claims the top spot as the largest continent in the world. With a population of more than 4.5 billion, it also has the most people in the world: 60 percent of all the people on Earth live here. The highest mountain on the planet is found in Asia, as well as the tallest building, the biggest city, and the stinkiest plant!

North Pacific Ocean

Admire the world's TALLEST WOODEN PAGODA (Shanxi, China)

Eat one of the world's MOST POISONOUS PUFFERFISH (Tokyo, Japan)

South Korea

Japan

Search for the SMALLEST DINOSAUR FOOTPRINTS (Gyeongsang Basin, South Korea)

China

Marvel at the world's BIGGEST CITY (Shanghai, China)

Paddle under the world's LARGEST NATURAL ARCH (Xianren Bridge, China)

Philippines

South China Sea

Vietnam   Step inside the LARGEST CAVE IN THE WORLD (Hang Son Doong, Vietnam)

Dive to the DEEPEST POINT IN THE OCEAN (Challenger Deep, Marianas Trench)

Singapore   Indonesia

Timor Leste

In times of danger, the entrances would have been sealed off by rolling huge circular stones across the doorways. These could only be opened from the inside.

It's likely that this underground city wasn't built for people to live in permanently, but as a place to shelter in times of war.

Today, about half of the underground city can be explored by visitors—but it's not for those with a fear of small spaces. Some of the corridors are VERY low and narrow.

There are about 600 hidden entrances to the buried city, so people on the surface could make a speedy escape below ground if danger threatened.

There are many other underground settlements in Cappadocia, some thousands of years old. Derinkuyu was once linked to another secret city, over five miles away, via a connecting tunnel.

The lower levels were carved out more recently than the upper levels, probably by Christians about 1,000 years ago. One of the largest chambers was an underground church.

TURKEY

Derinkuyu

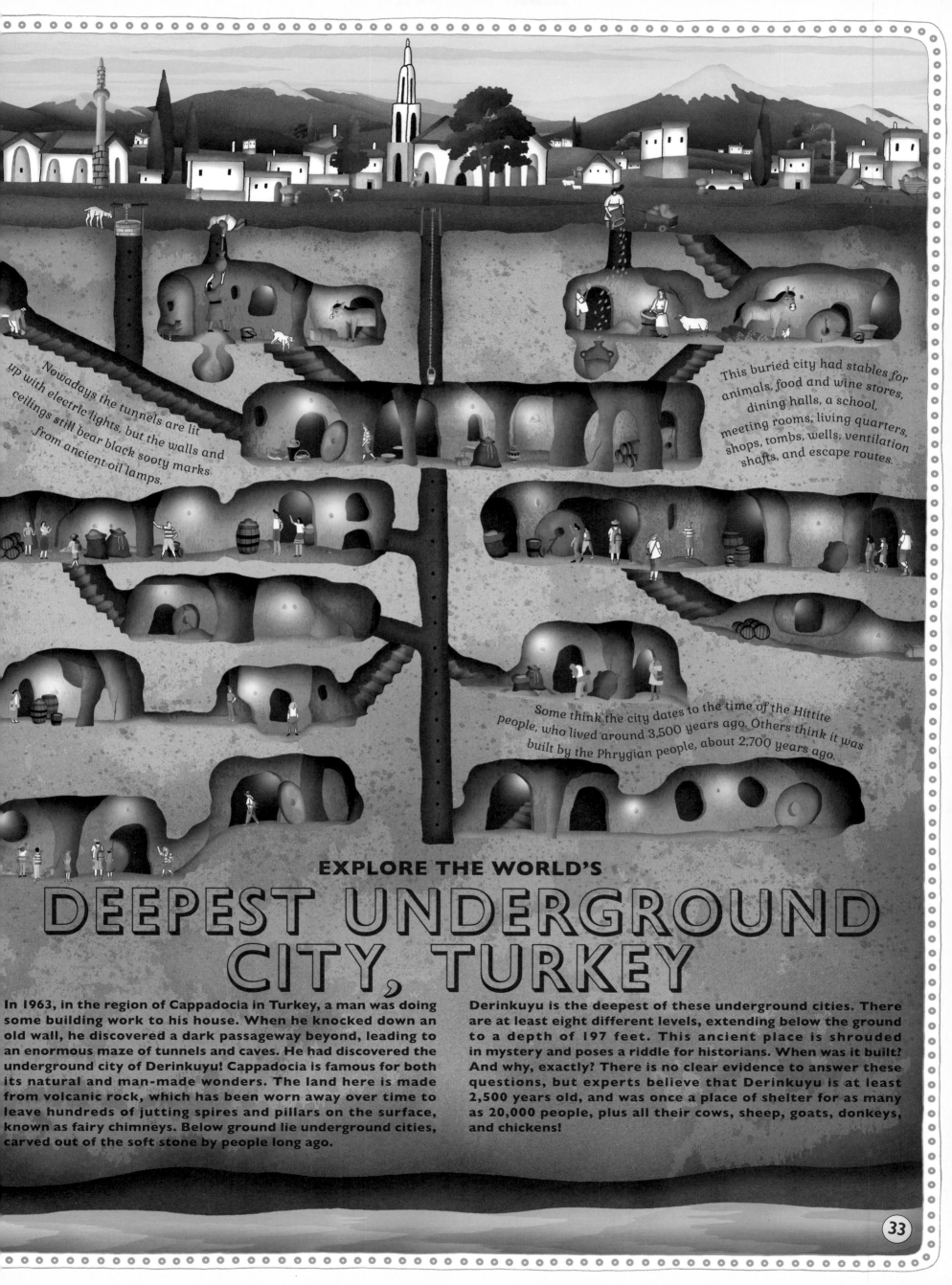

Nowadays the tunnels are lit up with electric lights, but the walls and ceilings still bear black sooty marks from ancient oil lamps.

This buried city had stables for animals, food and wine stores, dining halls, a school, meeting rooms, living quarters, shops, tombs, wells, ventilation shafts, and escape routes.

Some think the city dates to the time of the Hittite people, who lived around 3,500 years ago. Others think it was built by the Phrygian people, about 2,700 years ago.

EXPLORE THE WORLD'S
DEEPEST UNDERGROUND CITY, TURKEY

In 1963, in the region of Cappadocia in Turkey, a man was doing some building work to his house. When he knocked down an old wall, he discovered a dark passageway beyond, leading to an enormous maze of tunnels and caves. He had discovered the underground city of Derinkuyu! Cappadocia is famous for both its natural and man-made wonders. The land here is made from volcanic rock, which has been worn away over time to leave hundreds of jutting spires and pillars on the surface, known as fairy chimneys. Below ground lie underground cities, carved out of the soft stone by people long ago.

Derinkuyu is the deepest of these underground cities. There are at least eight different levels, extending below the ground to a depth of 197 feet. This ancient place is shrouded in mystery and poses a riddle for historians. When was it built? And why, exactly? There is no clear evidence to answer these questions, but experts believe that Derinkuyu is at least 2,500 years old, and was once a place of shelter for as many as 20,000 people, plus all their cows, sheep, goats, donkeys, and chickens!

TAKE A TRIP ON THE WORLD'S
LONGEST RAILWAY, RUSSIA

The Trans-Siberian Railway is the longest passenger railway on Earth, linking one side of the world's largest country to the other. The route begins in the Russian capital, Moscow, and ends in the port of Vladivostok on the Sea of Japan, 5,771 miles to the east. Imagine traveling on a train for seven days and nights, all within one single, enormous country. This record-breaking journey takes you across seven different time zones and through changing landscapes. The view from the window reveals lakes and rivers, mountains, forests, and grasslands.

This railway was the dream of Russia's last emperor, Tsar Nicholas II. He wanted to make it easier to move people and goods across his vast kingdom. However, for the railway's engineers, the mountainous shores of Lake Baikal—which lay right in the way—posed a problem. Eventually, they managed to build a track around the southern shore, but in the early days the entire train had to be hauled onto a special steam-powered ferry and shipped over the lake. During one particularly cold winter, tracks were even laid directly across the frozen ice!

Did you know, railways in different countries often have different width tracks? That's why it's rare for a single train to be able to take you such a long way.

Another record-breaker is Lake Baikal itself. Plunging to depths of 5,387 feet, it's the deepest lake in the world.

This ancient lake was formed by a huge rift in the Earth's crust between 20 and 25 million years ago. It's the oldest lake in the world, as well as the deepest!

The only species of freshwater seal on Earth, the Baikal seal, lives in this enormous lake.

Lake Baikal is the largest freshwater lake by volume, holding one fifth of all the fresh water on the planet (more than North America's Great Lakes combined).

Each carriage has its own conductor, the *provodnitsa*, who keeps everything in order.

Before the railway, people had to travel in stagecoaches, or sleighs in the winter, stopping every few miles to change horses. It was a slow process. Today, the railway transports several million passengers every year.

RUSSIA

Trans-Siberian Railway route

Moscow

Lake Baikal

Vladivostok

The Trans-Siberian Railway was built between 1891 and 1916. The workers had to contend with freezing weather, deadly diseases, and a shortage of building materials.

It took up to 90,000 laborers—most of them soldiers or prisoners—to complete the job. Teams started at either end of the route, working towards the middle.

Mongolian horses are small, but they are incredibly strong and tough. They can withstand freezing winters and scorching summers out on the open steppes.

The landscape is always changing. The route stretches across miles of rolling grasslands, as well as mountain passes, wooded hills, river-crossings and muddy marshlands.

The oldest winner was 70-year-old Bob Long, from the USA, who came first in 2019.

This race is so challenging that usually only about half of the 40 riders manage to complete it.

Marmots live in this part of the world, so the ground is littered with burrows. Luckily, the horses are experts at reading the lie of the land to avoid tripping up.

Riders are in the saddle from six in the morning until eight at night, for ten days in a row. It is exhausting work.

e route isn't marked, so riders have to navigate using a map and a GPS. They also have to carry a tracking device so the organizers can find them if they get lost!

Along the way, riders can choose to stay the night with local families or camp at a horse station.

Location of the Mongol Derby

MONGOLIA

In 2013, 19-year-old British rider Lara Prior-Palmer finished in just seven days, becoming the first woman, and the youngest ever participant, to win the race.

Riders expect to fall off their horses at least once.

SADDLE UP FOR THE

LONGEST HORSE RACE IN THE WORLD, MONGOLIA

This is no ordinary horse race. This is the longest, toughest horse race on Earth: the Mongol Derby. In this gruelling event, competitors from all over the world have to travel 621 miles across the vast landscapes of Mongolia. The race takes places over the course of ten days, with riders stopping every 25 miles to change horses. Participants have to ride 25 different Mongolian steeds—all of them semi-wild, and most of them prone to bucking, rearing, and bolting!

The Mongol Derby was inspired by the famous horse messenger system set up by the fearsome leader Genghis Khan in the 13th century. The Mongolian Empire was huge, and the ruler needed to communicate with his troops across great distances. To solve the problem, a network of post stations was built. A rider would carry a message 25 miles or so, then stop at a post station to switch to a fresh horse. In this way, a letter could travel 180 miles in a single day.

Birds that live in this remote wilderness include the white-browed rose finch, the upland buzzard, the Himalayan griffon, and the blood pheasant.

The 2002 kayaking expedit happened in late winter, whe the water level was lowest.

When the Yarlung Tsangpo enters India, it becomes the Brahmaputra River.

The Tsangpo Gorge is 17,390 feet deep: more than three times deeper than the Grand Canyon.

RIDING RAPIDS ON THE WORLD'S

HIGHEST RIVER, TIBET

Among the snowy peaks of the Himalayan Mountains is the source of the highest major river in the world: the Yarlung Tsangpo. With an average elevation of 13,100 feet, this river winds eastwards across Tibet. Where the river descends from the high Tibetan Plateau, it has carved out the Tsangpo Gorge: the deepest canyon in the world. The Yarlung Tsangpo is often called 'Tibet's Mother River'. But it is also nicknamed the 'Everest of Rivers' because of the risk posed to rafters and kayakers. With many dangerous rapids, only the bravest adventurers have tried to paddle along it. In 1993 a group of Japanese kayakers tried descending through the Tsangpo Gorge, but one of them was washed away. In 2002 a group of kayakers completed the upper gorge. So far, nobody has managed to kayak the whole length of the canyon, although many thrill-seekers dream about it.

The area's tricky terrain makes exploring the canyon a challenge for humans... but this means the wildlife here is largely undisturbed.

Kayakers have to contend with fierce rapids, vertical drops, swirling eddies, huge waves, and massive boulders.

The gorge has several waterfalls, including the 108-foot-tall Hidden Falls, which weren't widely known about until 1998.

The red goral is a mountain goat. It sleeps on narrow cliff ledges, out of reach of jackals and leopards.

Beneath the roof hole a small rainforest of trees and vines has grown.

The Sơn Đoòng cave has a total volume of about 1.4 BILLION cubic feet. That's the same size as is taken up by London's O2 arena... times 18!

Here, you'll find some of the tallest stalagmites in the world, measuring up to 262 feet high.

STEP INSIDE THE
LARGEST CAVE IN THE WORLD, VIETNAM

In 1991, deep in the forests of Vietnam, a local man named Hồ Khanh was walking through the jungle. He wasn't paying much attention to his surroundings when suddenly, he stopped short. At his feet was a vast, gaping hole. He could hear the roaring of a river far below, and he could see wisps of cloud escaping from the chasm. Hồ Khanh had discovered the entrance to what would turn out to be the largest cave on Earth.

Named Hang Sơn Đoòng, which means "Mountain River Cave," this enormous cavern was formed about three million years ago by water wearing away limestone rocks deep underground. It is so huge, you could park a Boeing 747 aircraft inside it, or a whole block of 40-story buildings. It's more than three miles long, 570 feet wide and a whopping 650 feet tall. The cave even has its own underground river, a lake, and a rainforest...

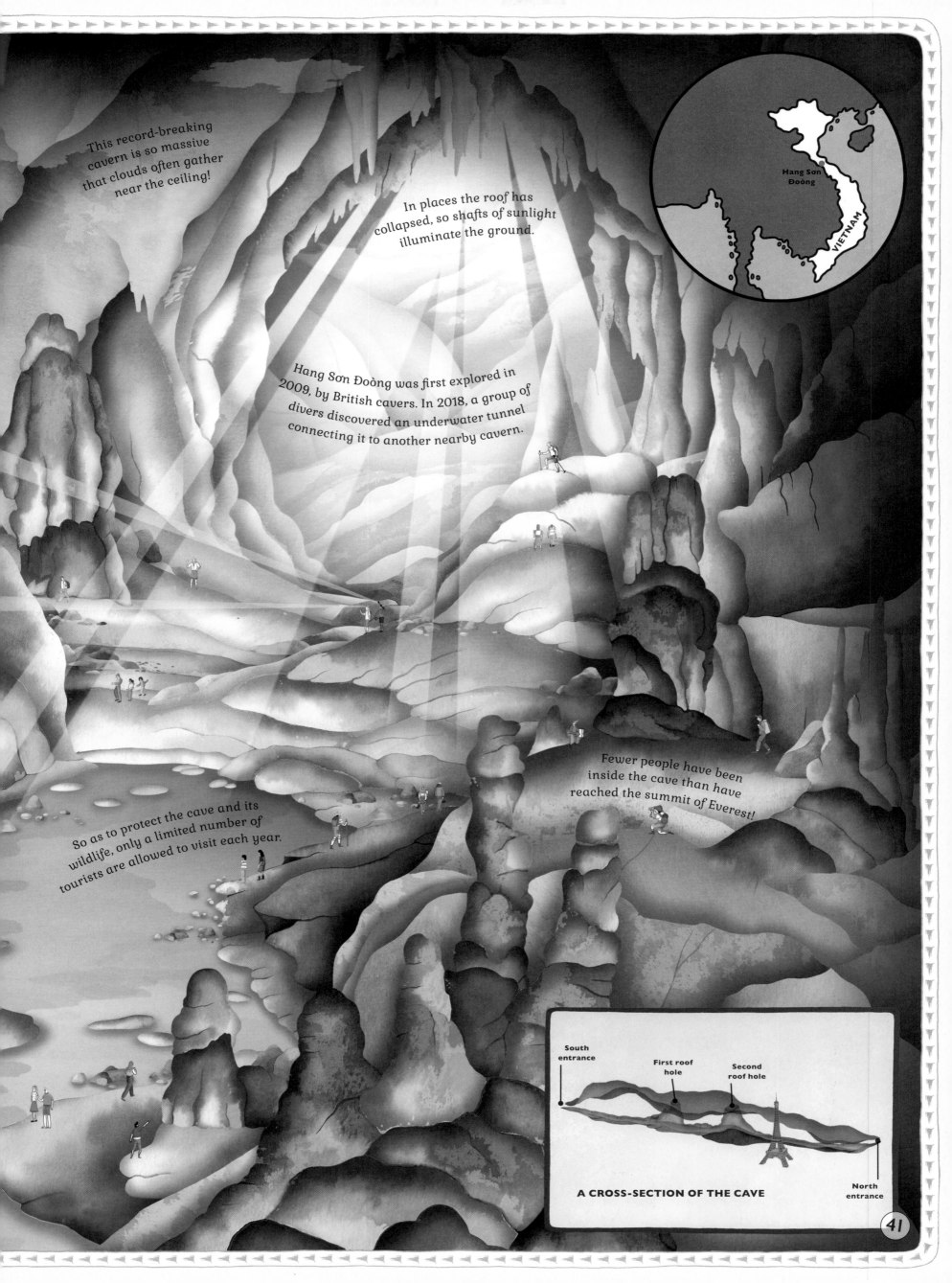

This record-breaking cavern is so massive that clouds often gather near the ceiling!

In places the roof has collapsed, so shafts of sunlight illuminate the ground.

VIETNAM

Hang Sơn Đoòng

Hang Sơn Đoòng was first explored in 2009, by British cavers. In 2018, a group of divers discovered an underwater tunnel connecting it to another nearby cavern.

Fewer people have been inside the cave than have reached the summit of Everest!

So as to protect the cave and its wildlife, only a limited number of tourists are allowed to visit each year.

South entrance

First roof hole

Second roof hole

North entrance

A CROSS-SECTION OF THE CAVE

SNIFF OUT THE WORLD'S
STINKIEST PLANT, INDONESIA

The titan arum is the rock star of the plant world. It's very rare. It's enormous. It only blooms once every few years. And it absolutely STINKS! When a titan arum comes into flower at a botanic garden, visitors flock in their thousands to get a glimpse... and a sniff! This extraordinary plant comes from the steamy, tropical rainforests of Sumatra, in Indonesia. It only blooms every five to ten years, and when it does, the huge, smelly flower only opens for about 36 hours before collapsing again.

It gives off such a foul stench that it has earned the nickname "corpse flower," or *bunga bangkai* in Indonesian. It is at its most stinky in the middle of the night, and smells like a disgusting mixture of decomposing flesh, strong cheese, sweaty socks, rotten cabbage, poop, and dead fish. You wouldn't think that this powerful odor was particularly attractive, but the smell does entice certain beetles and flies that like to eat rotting meat. Delicious!

The flying fox is one of the largest b— in the world, with a wingspan of up to five feet.

It can take up to ten years for these plants to store up the energy to produce such a huge flower.

Keep your eyes peeled in the jungles of Sumatra for the Sunda clouded leopard. This rare, secretive cat is an excellent climber.

Siamang gibbons are famous for their loud territorial screams and barks, which can be heard for miles around.

When the titan arum flowers, it warms up. This causes the air around it to rise, which sends its signature stink far and wide throughout the fore—

Large central spike is called the "spadix"

The "spathe" is a large, petal-like leaf

3 METERS

The titan arum is the tallest flower in the world. Blooms can reach over nine feet tall and grow six inches per day.

Carrion beetles love rotting meat and are lured by the smell of the foul flower. They get covered in pollen, which they transfer to the next flower on their travels, helping the plant to grow seeds.

INDONESIA

This plant wasn't widely known about until a botanist sent a seedling to Kew Gardens in 1878. When it flowered in 1926, it caused such a stir that the police were called in to control the crowds!

The fire-tufted barbet is difficult to spot, as its green feathers help it blend in with the jungle foliage.

AUSTRALASIA & OCEANIA

The planet's smallest continent is a big-hitter where record-breaking wildlife is concerned. Off the east coast of Australia is the Great Barrier Reef: the world's largest coral reef—in fact, the largest living structure on Earth. Elsewhere in Australasia you'll discover the most spectacular cave of glow-worms and the greatest insect builders... but watch out for the world's biggest crocodile!

Swim away from the MOST VENOMOUS JELLYFISH (Box Jellyfish, Papua New Guinea)

Spot the BIGGEST BUTTERFLY (Queen Alexandra's Birdwing, Papua New Guinea)

Papua New Guinea

Indonesia

Discover the nearly 6-foot-long BIGGEST DINOSAUR FOOTPRINTS (Broome, Australia)

Meet the GREATEST INSECT BUILDERS (Termites, Australia)

Catch up with the FASTEST FISH IN THE WORLD (Black Marlin, Australia)

Australia

Take a trip on AUSTRALIA'S LONGEST STRAIGHT ROAD (Eyre Highway, Southern Australia)

90 MILES LONG

Witness the world's BIGGEST GATHERING OF BUDGIES (Alice Springs, Central Australia)

Snorkel the world's LARGEST CORAL REEF (Great Barrier Reef, Australia)

Measure the bill of the BIRD WITH THE LONGEST BEAK (Australian Pelican, Australia)

Ride on the 138-foot LONGEST BICYCLE IN THE WORLD (Adelaide, Australia)

Tasmania

Visit the tiny mining town where the 145-pound BIGGEST GOLD NUGGET EVER DISCOVERED was found in 1869 (Moliagul, Australia)

Indian Ocean

Tasman Sea

Hawaiian Islands

Shelter from the half-inch-wide BIGGEST RAINDROPS on Earth (Measured in 1999, Marshall Islands)

Stand on top of the world's TALLEST MOUNTAIN, measured from seabed to peak (Mauna Kea, Hawaii)

Federated States of Micronesia

Marshall Islands

Pacific Ocean

Solomon Islands

Steer clear of the world's LARGEST CROCODILE (Saltwater Crocodile, Solomon Islands)

Tuvalu

Beat the record for the FASTEST COCONUT TREE CLIMB (Tahiti, French Polynesia)

Vanuatu

Samoa

New Caledonia

Fiji

French Polynesia

Bathe in the LARGEST LAGOON (New Caledonia)

See the light at the world's MOST SPECTACULAR GLOW-WORM CAVE (Waitomo Caves, New Zealand)

Tonga

Norfolk Island

Kermadec Islands

Listen out for the world's HEAVIEST PARROT (Kakapo, New Zealand)

New Zealand

Stop off at the world's MOST SOUTHERLY CAPITAL CITY (Wellington, New Zealand)

Black marlin have excellent eyesight, allowing them to keep track of the quick, darting movements of their prey.

Sometimes, marlin have been spotted leaping above the surface of the ocean.

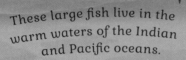

Black marlin habitat

AUSTRALIA

These large fish live in the warm waters of the Indian and Pacific oceans.

CATCH UP WITH THE

FASTEST FISH IN THE WORLD, AUSTRALIA

It's not easy measuring how fast a fish can swim. But if there were an Underwater Olympics, the black marlin would probably win gold for speed. Its top speed is thought to lie somewhere in the region of 80 miles per hour! For comparison, that's more than 20 times faster than the quickest human swimmer. So how does the marlin reach such super speeds? Its sleek body is perfectly suited to life in the fast lane: its sharp bill cuts through the water, followed by its smooth, streamlined body. Its huge, muscular tail works like an engine, powering the fish along.

Every year, between October and December, black marlin gather in large groups to lay their eggs in the waters around the Great Barrier Reef. Here, these expert hunters feed on shoals of tuna and mackerel, ramming prey with their fearsome bills, to stun them. But although they are quick, the marlin still need to be on the lookout. They themselves are hunted by other super-fast predators, such as the deadly mako shark.

The marlin's speed was calculated by measuring how fast the fish pulled fishing line off a reel on a fishing boat. But it's not exact, because the boat's speed and the current can alter how fast the line unravels.

Scientists worry that warming ocean temperatures are leading to lower levels of oxygen in deep waters. This means that marlin are tending to stay nearer the surface, making them more vulnerable to fishing boats.

Fishing crews have reported catching mako sharks with marlin bills embedded in them.

As well as being speedy, marlin can cover huge distances. One fish was tracked swimming from California to New Zealand... over 9,900 miles away!

The mako shark is one of the marlin's top predators. This speedy hunter has been described as a torpedo with teeth!

Marlin are among the biggest bony fish on the planet. The largest females can grow to over 13 feet and weigh up to 1,540 pounds: that's heavier than a polar bear.

MORE SPEEDY SWIMMERS

Sailfish: Top speed 68 miles per hour

Striped marlin: Top speed 50 miles per hour

Mako shark: Top speed 46 miles per hour

Termite mounds can stand for hundreds—if not thousands—of years. If a mound becomes damaged, workers rush to the area to make repairs.

Most termites live for a year or two, but the queen of the African mound-building termite can survive for up to 60 years, making her the longest-living insect on Earth!

The queen's job is to lay up to 30,000 eggs every day! Her enormous body is so big that she can't move. Workers do everything for her.

A termite mound has a central chimney, as well as smaller ventilation shafts. It contains a queen's chamber, nurseries, fungus gardens, and pantries.

Northern Territory

Litchfield National Park

AUSTRALIA

MEET THE
GREATEST INSECT BUILDERS, AUSTRALIA

There are more than 2,000 different species of termite in the world. Not all of them build mounds—some live in other types of nest.

Termites are the master-builders of the animal world. These insects are tiny: some no bigger than a grain of rice. But, working together, they can build enormous mounds up to 26 feet high: by far the largest structures made by insects. In Australia's Northern Territory, many sky-scraping mounds dot the landscape. The termites build their amazing structures out of a mixture of clay, spit, and poop. These colonies are incredible feats of engineering. No single termite is in charge of the building project, yet each worker somehow knows what to do. Below ground, a termite nest extends in a maze of chambers and passageways. The mound on top is the tip of the iceberg, acting like a cross between a giant lung and an air-conditioning unit. The walls are covered in tiny holes allowing air to pass in and out, so the termites always have a fresh supply. The mound has a network of ventilation shafts to keep the nest cool and moist: just the way the termites like it. In fact, human architects have been inspired by termite mounds to design self-cooling buildings.

Workers set out from the mound to find grass to eat. They return full of chewed-up grass, which they poop out. Other workers use this grassy compost to build fungus farms.

Ants try to raid the termite nests. Soldier termites guard the mound, fighting off ants with their pincers.

Inside the mound the termites grow a special type of fungus. This fungus helps them break down the plants they eat, so they are easier to digest.

TYPES OF TERMITES

King

Worker

Soldier

Queen

More than a million mound-building termites can live in a single nest. A termite colony includes a queen, a king, workers, and soldiers.

THE LIFE-CYCLE OF A NEW ZEALAND GLOW-WORM

Egg (3 weeks)

Adult fly (lives for only 3 days)

Glowing larva (6–12 months)

Pupa (2 weeks)

There are several different types of glow-worm around the world: some are the larvae of flies, like Waitomo's glow-worms. Others are beetle larvae.

The blue-green light is caused by a chemical reaction inside the glow-worm's tail. Glowing creatures are called "bioluminescent."

The more hungry a glow-worm is, the brighter it glows!

SEE THE LIGHT AT THE WORLD'S
MOST SPECTACULAR GLOW-WORM CAVE, NEW ZEALAND

In 1887 on the North Island of New Zealand, a local Maori chief named Tane Tinorau and an English surveyor named Frederick Mace together explored a labyrinth of limestone caves. On a small raft, they paddled along an underground river, using candles to light their way. They were amazed by what they discovered: a huge cavern, the ceiling twinkling with thousands of tiny lights... glow-worms. The Waitomo Caves have since become world famous, attracting visitors from around the globe to marvel at this galaxy of living stars.

But, although they look beautiful, Waitomo's glow-worms aren't as peaceful as they may seem. They aren't actually worms at all, but are the larvae (the baby, maggot-like forms) of a type of fly. Once they hatch from their eggs, these little maggots are hungry. They begin to glow, lighting up their bodies to attract other insects, such as moths and midges. When this prey draws near, it becomes trapped by the sticky, slimy threads that dangle from the glow-worms. Then, the prey is reeled in, punctured, and slurped up. Delicious!

This type of glow-worm is found only in New Zealand. Its Latin name, Arachnocampa, means "spider-worm," because of the way it snares its prey in a sticky web.

The Waitomo Caves are millions of years old. They were formed by water running along cracks in the limestone rocks gradually hollowing out caverns and passageways.

North Island

Waitomo

NEW ZEALAND

The glowing larvae live for between six and twelve months. Once they have fed enough, they transform into flies, mate, and then die.

Over thousands of years, stalactites and stalagmites are formed by water dripping from the ceiling and depositing tiny bits of limestone.

A stalactite hangs from the ceiling and a stalagmite grows upwards from the floor. They grow roughly half an inch every 100 years!

The glow-worms are tiny at first, but can grow up to four centimetres long: about the length of a matchstick.

51

NEW ZEALAND

Codfish
Island

South
Island

Several hundred years ago, human settlers introduced new predators to New Zealand, including cats and rats. These creatures hunted the flightless, defenseless kakapos almost to extinction.

Kakapos can live for 90 years, making them one of the world's longest-living birds!

Kakapos use their strong legs to waddle through the undergrowth. It sometimes looks as though they're jogging!

Today, there are only about 200 kakapos left in the wild. But, thanks to some dedicated conservation efforts, their numbers are slowly increasing.

LISTEN OUT FOR THE WORLD'S
HEAVIEST PARROT, NEW ZEALÅND

"Kakapo" means "night parrot" in the Maori language. These birds come out at night to search for berries and seeds to eat.

On a remote island off the south coast of New Zealand lives a very peculiar parrot: the kakapo. This gentle, friendly bird holds a few world records. Not only is it the heaviest species of parrot on Earth, weighing up to nine pounds, it is also the world's only flightless parrot, as well as being the only nocturnal parrot. The kakapo is one of the world's longest-living birds and, if that wasn't enough, it is also one of the world's noisiest birds!

Once widespread throughout New Zealand, these precious parrots now exist only on a few tiny islands, where they are protected from predators. In the breeding season, the male's loud calls can be heard echoing across the forested hills. He chooses a high piece of land, hollows out a shallow bowl for himself to sit in, then takes his position. From here, he will send out booming calls to attract a female. These calls can be heard from over three miles away!

Codfish Island, where most of the world's kakapos live, has been set aside as a predator-free bird sanctuary. Here, experts help protect and conserve these rare birds.

Although they can't fly, kakapos are good climbers. Sometimes they can be found perching 65 feet high in the branches of a tree.

The male kakapo makes his booming call using special air sacs in his chest.

The male's mating serenade can last eight hours. He repeats it every night for two or three months.

Owl-like face

Green feathers for camouflage among the undergrowth

Circle of feathers around each eye funnels sound towards the ears

Wings aren't used for flight, but to help the kakapo balance

Arctic Ocean

Greenland

Alaska (USA)

Battle blizzards on the COLDEST ENDURANCE RUN (Arctic Ultra Marathon, Yukon, Canada)

Brave the heights of the 4,100-foot STEEPEST, TALLEST CLIFF (Mount Thor, Nunavut, Canada)

Gulf of Alaska

Canada

Trek part of the LONGEST COASTLINE IN THE WORLD (Canada)

Hudson Bay

Groove at the world's LARGEST JAZZ FESTIVAL (Montreal, Canada)

Jump into the world's LARGEST FRESHWATER LAKE (Lake Superior, Canada)

Climb one of the TALLEST TREES in the world (Coast Redwood, California, USA)

United States of America

Stay cool at the HOTTEST PLACE IN THE USA (Death Valley, California, USA)

Meet the man with THE MOST WORLD RECORDS (Ashrita Furman, New York, USA)

Pat the WORLD'S TALLEST HORSE (Big Jake, Michigan, USA)

North Pacific Ocean

Raft along the world's LONGEST CANYON (Grand Canyon, Arizona, USA)

Dig dirt on the LARGEST MAMMAL COLONY (Prairie Dogs, Texas, USA)

Walk the LONGEST HIKING ROUTE (Appalachian Trail, Western USA)

The Bahamas

Spot the tiny creature that survives A LIFETIME WITHOUT WATER (Kangaroo Rat, Sonoran Desert, Mexico)

Get in a flap with the BIGGEST COLONY OF BATS (Bracken Cave, Texas, USA)

Mexico

Gulf of Mexico

Cuba

Discover the world's LARGEST CRYSTALS (Cave of Giant Crystals, Mexico)

Watch the birds at the world's LARGEST CAVE SHAFT (Cave of Swallows, Mexico)

NORTH AMERICA

North America has some spectacular natural record-breakers. Here, you can check out the world's largest lake and tallest trees, as well as the most enormous cave shaft on Earth. This diverse continent is also home to some extraordinary human record-breakers, including a man from New York, Ashrita Furman, who holds more Guinness World Records than anyone else on the planet!

brador Sea

Blink and you'll miss the world's FASTEST BIRD (Peregrine Falcon, New York, USA)

North Atlantic Ocean

Azores

Bermuda

Don't touch the MOST DEADLY TREE (Manchineel Tree, The Bahamas)

Sargasso Sea

Caribbean Sea

Relax on the world's BIGGEST CRUISE SHIP (Symphony of the Seas, Caribbean)

Many birds, such as geese and hawks, stop here for a break on their annual migrations.

Compared to Russia's ancient Lake Baikal, which is around 25 million years old, Lake Superior is fairly young. It was carved out during the last ice age, about 10,000 years ago.

CANADA

USA

Great Lakes

This gigantic lake is so huge that in summer, the sun sets 35 minutes later on the western shore than at the eastern tip.

More than 200 rivers run into Lake Superior: it holds about a tenth of the world's surface fresh water.

JUMP INTO THE WORLD'S
LARGEST FRESHWATER LAKE, CANADA

Lake Superior is well named. It is superior to all other freshwater lakes in size, with an area of 31,700 square miles: roughly the same size as Ireland. Lying between Canada and the USA, this vast body of water is the largest of North America's Great Lakes—it is so big that it could hold all the water from the other four Great Lakes combined. And here's another mind-boggling fact: if you took the water in Lake Superior and spread it out, there would be enough to cover the whole of North and South America in a puddle

12 inches deep! That's because the lake holds three quadrillion gallons of water. (And yes, that is a real number: it's a three with 15 zeros after it.)

Much of the lake is frozen over in winter but by the summer the ice has melted and you can go for a dip. But taking the plunge here is not for the faint-hearted: it's chilly! Lake Superior is the northernmost and coldest of the Great Lakes, with an average year-round temperature of just over 39°F. Brrrr!

There are about 550 known shipwrecks in these depths, which are well preserved by the cool, non-salty water.

These waters are home to about 88 species of fish, including the enormous lake sturgeon, which can grow to more than six feet long.

Lake Superior's largest island is Isle Royal, in the state of Michigan, USA. The island has its own lakes, which have their own islands. So you could stand on an island in a little lake on a big island in a big lake!

If you straightened out the lake's 1,825-mile-long shoreline, it could stretch from Canada to Ireland.

The lake's deepest point is nearly 1,280 feet down: you could drop New York's Empire State Building into the water and only its pinnacle would poke above the surface.

The Caspian Sea—a landlocked saltwater sea between Asia and Europe—is even bigger than Lake Superior. It is sometimes classed as the world's biggest lake.

The Great Lakes

CANADA

USA

Lake Superior

Lake Huron

Lake Michigan

Lake Erie

Lake Ontario

New York City is home to many pairs of falcons: in fact, it has the highest concentration of nesting peregrines anywhere on Earth.

In the 1960s, peregrine falcons were nearly wiped out in the eastern USA because farmers' pesticides poisoned the food chain. Thanks to a special breeding program, they are now thriving.

Peregrine falcons can be found all over New York, on apartment blocks, bridges, and even at the top of the tallest skyscrapers!

The word "peregrine" means "wanderer." Some migrate up to 15,500 miles a year in search of warm weather.

The fastest falcon dive ever recorded took place in 2005, and measured an eye-watering 241 miles per hour.

With eyes on the sides of its head, a pigeon can scan the skies to keep a lookout for danger. It dodges and darts to evade the falcon's clutches.

USA

New York City

BLINK AND YOU'LL MISS THE WORLD'S
FASTEST BIRD, USA

Among the gleaming skyscrapers of New York, several hundred feet above the busy streets, live a group of surprising residents: peregrine falcons. The lofty buildings provide nesting sites and perches for these formidable hunters, who normally live on craggy cliff-faces. In the city, currents of air are funneled up the sides of the high towers, lifting the birds skywards.

When a peregrine falcon dives for prey, it is the fastest animal on the planet, reaching speeds of more than 180 miles per hour. These birds hunt pigeons: another cliff-dwelling creature that has found a home in the city. But they also prey on songbirds, and even parakeets and other escaped pets. A falcon hunts from the air, rising above its victim then tucking in its wings and plummeting in a swift, steep dive. It strikes with deadly force, stunning prey before snaring it with its talons.

New York City is also home to Ashrita Furman: the person with the most Guinness World Records on the planet. During his lifetime he has set more than 700 records...

...These include many bizarre feats, such as underwater pogo-stick jumping, catching ping-pong balls using chopsticks, and balancing a lawn mower on his chin!

Birds and skyscrapers don't always mix: sadly, about 90,000 birds die each year in New York City from crashing into windows after being confused by reflections in the glass.

Eyesight is eight times more powerful than human vision: the falcon can spot a pigeon from nearly two miles away!

Long, pointed wings can be folded back when diving

Sleek, teardrop-shaped body slices through the air

Transparent third eyelid protects the eyes when diving, like a pair of goggles

59

General Sherman
(Giant Sequoia)
315 feet

Big Ben
275 feet

Hyperion
(Coast Redwood)
380 feet

These huge trees are high-rise habitats for other plants. Mosses, lichens, ferns, berry bushes, and even other small trees grow among the branches.

Many animals shelter in the redwoods, including raccoons, voles, pine martens, northern-spotted owls, and numerous insects.

Coast redwoods are among the oldest living things on Earth. Some are more than 2,000 years old, meaning they were around during the Roman Empire!

CLIMB ONE OF THE
TALLEST TREES IN THE WORLD, USA

You're not normally allowed to climb coast redwoods because these majestic trees are protected. But at certain times of year in the Santa Cruz Mountains of California, a small number of climbers are allowed to ascend into the canopy (with the help of a safety harness and an experienced guide). It's a breathtaking view from the top, as the coast redwood is the tallest type of tree in the world. These towering giants can reach dizzying heights of over 328 feet: the same as a 30-story building.

The tallest individual tree on Earth lives somewhere in Redwood National Park, California. Its exact location is kept a secret by park rangers, so the tree doesn't get damaged by stampeding tourists. This record-busting tree, called Hyperion, measures nearly 380 feet tall: 65 feet taller than London's Big Ben clock tower. And it's still growing. Coast redwoods are famously long-living, and—at a mere 600 years old (about 20 in human years)—Hyperion is just a youngster!

The oldest living tree in the world is thought to be Methuselah, a bristlecone pine from the White Mountains in California, estimated to be more than 4,800 years old.

It is illegal to climb these trees without special permission. It is likely that more people have reached the top of Everest than the top of a coast redwood tree!

In India there is a 550-year-old giant banyan tree with a perimeter of 2,776 feet, giving it the biggest tree canopy in the world.

Coast Redwood habitat

USA

California

For hundreds of years, scientists didn't know where the marbled murrelet bird nested. In the 1970s, these rare creatures were found living in coast redwoods.

The biggest tree on Earth by volume is General Sherman: a giant sequoia from California's Sequoia National Park. Its trunk has a circumference of 101 feet!

Redwoods grow tall thanks to the mild climate and fertile soil here. They like the summer fogs, which keep their leaves moist. Their thick bark can even protect them from forest fires.

DIG THE DIRT ON THE
LARGEST EVER COLONY OF MAMMALS, USA

Prairie dogs are furry, burrowing animals that live on the grasslands of the western USA. In 1901, in the state of Texas, ranchers came across an enormous colony of black-tailed prairie dogs. It measured a gigantic 248 miles long by 99 miles wide, covering roughly 25,000 square miles, which is about three times the size of Wales! This prairie dog town was home to around 400 million creatures, and was the largest colony of mammals, by area, ever discovered.

At the time, the USA was absolutely teeming with prairie dogs: there were billions of them. But sadly for the prairie dogs, they were seen as pests by farmers, so many were killed during the 20th century. This record-breaking colony no longer exists, but many national parks in the USA now protect these sociable creatures. Keep an eye out for prairie dogs nibbling the grass, watching for predators, play-fighting, and even kissing to say hello!

Prairie dog towns have lots of family burrows. Each burrow has several chambers, including one near the surface where the animals can keep an ear out for goings-on above ground.

The colony work as a team: while some feed or burrow, others keep a lookout for danger.

To greet each other, prairie dogs sometimes kiss on the mouth, touching teeth. This helps them work out whether they know each other.

Prairie dogs aren't actually dogs: they're related to squirrels. They get their name from their call, which sounds like a dog bark.

Over one foot long (same size as a rabbit)

Short, strong legs with long claws, for burrowing

Light brown hair for camouflage against muddy mounds

Prairie dogs have lots of predators, including coyotes, bobcats, eagles, hawks, rattlesnakes, and black-footed ferrets.

USA

Black-tailed prairie dog habitat

Burrowing owls sometimes move into empty prairie dog tunnels.

Prairie dogs crop the grass nearby to keep a clear lookout for predators. Farmers don't like this, which is why many prairie dog colonies have been destroyed.

Fun-loving young pups spend their days wrestling and play-fighting.

Prairie dogs are brilliant communicators. They have many different chirps, barks, and yips, which mean different things: their warning calls even vary depending on what kind of predator is approaching.

A colony can have hundreds or even thousands of prairie dogs. A small family group in a colony is called a coterie.

DO NOT TOUCH THE WORLD'S
MOST DEADLY TREE, THE BAHAMAS

When strolling along a beautiful beach in the Caribbean, don't be deceived by the tempting fruits of the manchineel tree. Although they look like apples, good enough to eat, be warned: a single bite can cause agony and may prove fatal. At first, the fruit tastes good—sweet and slightly peppery. But then it starts to burn, causing your throat to swell up. Soon, you won't be able to eat, talk... or perhaps even breathe. But these poison apples are actually the least toxic part of the tree. The sap is even deadlier.

The manchineel tree has a thick, milky sap that oozes from its branches and leaves. This toxic slime can burn like acid, making human skin bubble and blister. Never shelter under a manchineel tree in a downpour, because the water droplets will wash the noxious sap onto your skin, causing a whole lot of pain. If even a tiny bit of the sap gets in your eyes it can cause blindness. So don't eat the fruit. Don't touch the sap. Don't climb the tree. And don't stand under it in the rain!

These dangerous trees grow along the tropical coastlines of the Caribbean, Mexico, Central America, and Florida.

Beware... the toxic smoke from a burning manchineel tree can lead to breathing difficulties and eye problems.

In the 16th century, Spanish explorers who came across the fatal fruit of the manchineel tree called it la manzanilla de la muerte, which means "the little apple of death."

Every part of the tree, from the fruit and sap to the leaves and bark, is poisonous.

This tree is not only harmful to humans, it is also poisonous to other mammals and birds.

The fruit of the manchineel tree looks similar to a crab apple.

THE
BAHAMAS

CARIBBEAN
SEA

One of the only creatures that seems immune is the black-spined iguana. This daring reptile can live among the branches and eat the fruit.

Many manchineel trees are marked with an "X" to signal danger.

The blue land crab also sometimes eats these toxic apples. Local stories tell of people being poisoned after feasting on the meat of manchineel-eating crabs.

The dripping sap can damage the paint of any cars left parked in the manchineel's shade.

WATCH THE BIRDS AT THE WORLD'S
LARGEST CAVE SHAFT, MEXICO

In the tropical jungles of Mexico lies a remarkable wonder of the natural world: the Cave of Swallows. A huge hole in the forest floor, the cave opens up like a gaping mouth. It is so big that its size is almost impossible to get your head around. From the rim of the pit, there is a sheer drop of 1,233 feet to the floor below. If you took a tumble over the edge, it would take at least ten seconds for you to hit the ground. Try counting this out loud—it's a long way to fall!

This huge pit is the largest known cave shaft in the world, deep enough to swallow the Eiffel Tower, with a bit of room to spare. Once you're inside, it expands into a huge cavern: the floor is about the size of three soccer fields end to end. Thousands of birds nest on ledges on the craggy walls. Each morning at sunrise, they fly upwards, swooping in circles as they ascend out of the cave. They return to roost in the evening as the light fades from the sky. It's a spectacular sight.

Despite the cave's name, the birds that live here aren't swallows, but white-collared swifts. Flocks of green parakeets also make their home on the rocky walls.

Cave mouth

Ground level

Floor of sinkhole

Birds of prey, such as falcons, lurk near the cave mouth to pick off the swifts as they emerge.

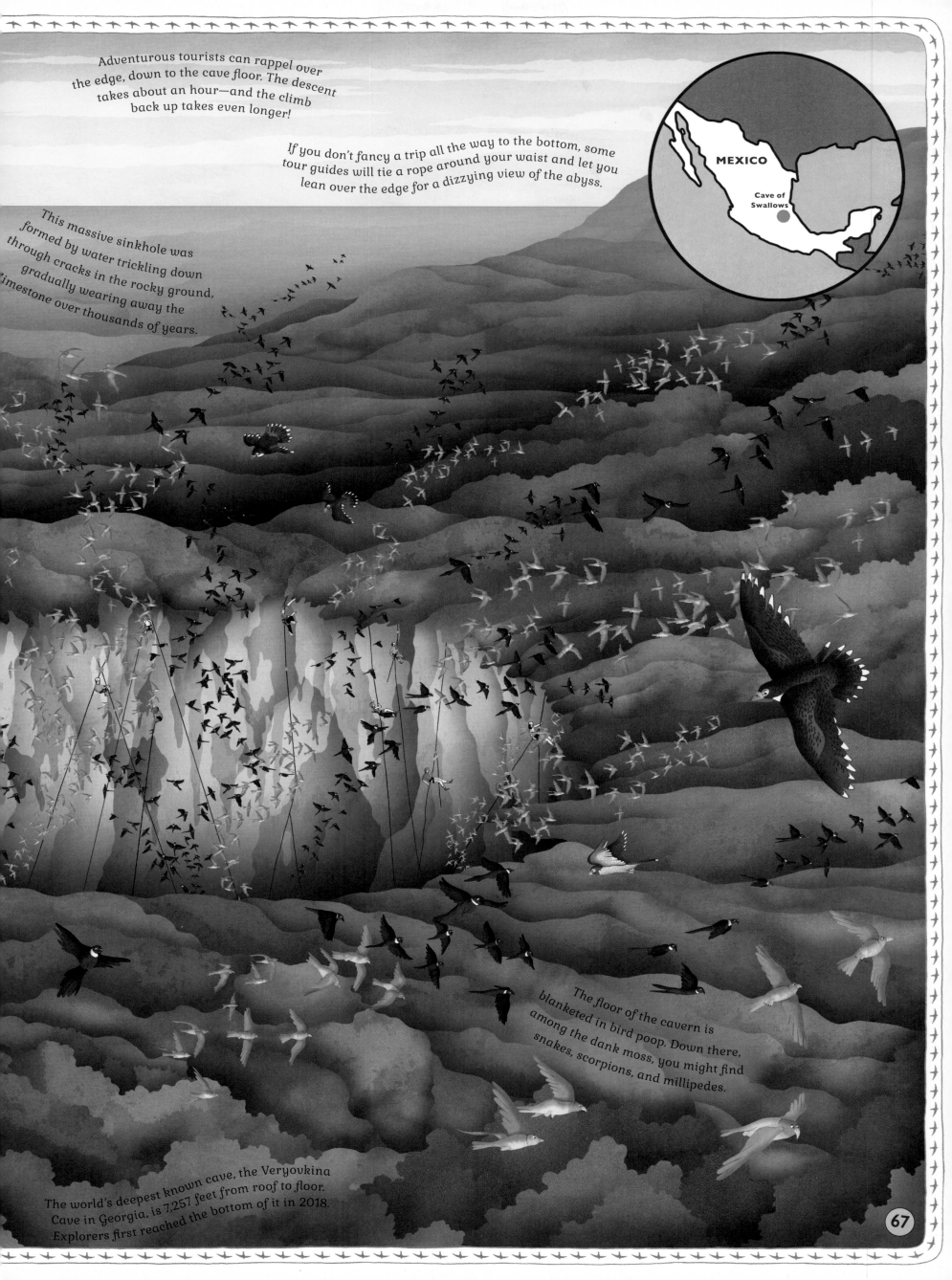

Adventurous tourists can rappel over the edge, down to the cave floor. The descent takes about an hour—and the climb back up takes even longer!

If you don't fancy a trip all the way to the bottom, some tour guides will tie a rope around your waist and let you lean over the edge for a dizzying view of the abyss.

MEXICO

Cave of Swallows

This massive sinkhole was formed by water trickling down through cracks in the rocky ground, gradually wearing away the limestone over thousands of years.

The floor of the cavern is blanketed in bird poop. Down there, among the dank moss, you might find snakes, scorpions, and millipedes.

The world's deepest known cave, the Veryovkina Cave in Georgia, is 7,257 feet from roof to floor. Explorers first reached the bottom of it in 2018.

Mexico

Honduras

Guatemala

Belize

El Salvador

Nicaragua

Costa Rica

Panama

Cuba

Haiti

Dominican Republic

Caribbean Sea

Spot the SMALLEST BIRD (Bee Hummingbird, Cuba)

Feel the spray of the TALLEST WATERFALL (Angel Falls, Venezuela)

Take it easy with the world's SLOWEST-MOVING MAMMAL (Three-Toed Sloth, Panama)

Brace yourself for the most PAINFUL INSECT STING (Bullet Ant, Nicaragua)

Marvel at the EVERLASTING LIGHTNING STORM (Lake Maracaibo, Venezuela)

Buy an umbrella in the RAINIEST CITY on Earth (Quibdó, Colombia)

Venezuela

French Gui

Guyana

Suriname

Watch out for the world's MOST POISONOUS CREATURE (Golden Poison Frog, Colombia)

Admire the MOST ENORMOUS SPECIES OF TORTOISE (Galápagos Giant Tortoise, Galápagos Islands)

Colombia

Ecuador

Hear the call of the world's LOUDEST LAND ANIMAL (Howler Monkey, Peru)

Explore the BIGGEST RAINFOREST (The Amazon Rainforest)

Hold your nose for the SMELLIEST BIRD (Hoatzin, Bolivia)

Peru

South Pacific Ocean

Be impressed by the world's BIGGEST GEOGLYPHS (Nazca Lines, Peru)

Adjust to the altitude in the HIGHEST PERMANENT HUMAN SETTLEMENT (La Rinconada, Peru)

Bolivia

Paraguay

Survive in the DRIEST DESERT (Atacama Desert, Chile)

Go horse-riding in the LONGEST MOUNTAIN RANGE (The Andes)

Chile

Argentina

Uraguay

Discover the LARGEST DINOSAUR EVER TO WALK THE EARTH (Argentinosaurus, Argentina)

Falkland Islands

CENTRAL & SOUTH AMERICA

This continent is famous for its wildlife, so it's no surprise that it is home to some amazing record-breaking creatures, from highly poisonous frogs to enormous snakes. Aside from its animals, South America has many superlative natural features, from the world's largest river to the biggest rainforest to the longest mountain range.

Check out the ten-foot-wide LARGEST WATER LILIES (Victoria Water Lilies, Guyana)

Paddle down the BIGGEST RIVER IN THE WORLD (The Amazon River)

Applaud the LARGEST PARADE OF KITE SURFERS (Praia do Cumbuco, Brazil)

Brazil

Avoid becoming the dinner of the LARGEST SNAKE (Green Anaconda, Brazil)

Steer clear of the DEADLIEST ISLAND on Earth (Snake Island, Brazil)

South Atlantic Ocean

COLOMBIA

Golden
poison
frog
habitat

Poison dart frogs in captivity aren't as poisonous as those in the wild. This is probably because they have a different diet.

Only one specific type of fire-bellied snake seems immune to this frog's poison. The snake can stomach a meal that would kill most other predators.

Poison dart frogs are small but deadly. The golden poison frog is one of the largest species, measuring only two inches long.

WATCH OUT FOR THE WORLD'S
MOST POISONOUS CREATURE, COLOMBIA

Deep in the jungles of Colombia, you might be lucky (or unlucky...) enough to come across the most poisonous creature known to science: the golden poison frog. This miniature frog may look harmless, but it contains enough poison to kill ten adult men, two African elephants, or 22,000 mice! This tiny terror lives on the floor of the rainforest, near streams and ponds, keeping moist among the damp leaves. Its bright color warns any predators considering taking a bite to think again. With poisonous frogs, the brighter the color, the stronger the poison.

If you were to hold one in your bare hand for too long, the frog's toxins could seep into your bloodstream through your skin, causing paralysis and heart failure within minutes. For centuries, the Embera people of Colombia made poison darts by rubbing them across the frog's back. These darts were then fired from blowpipes to hunt birds and monkeys. Once laced with poison, they would remain toxic for two years!

A GALLERY OF POISON DART FROGS

Blue poison dart frog

Green-and-black poison dart frog

Blue jeans poison frog

Three-striped poison dart frog

Dyeing dart frog

Strawberry poison dart frog

SCALE OF THE GOLDEN POISON FROG

This jewel-like frog most likely gets its poison from the beetles it eats, which get their poison from plants in their diet. Inside the frog, the strength of the poison is boosted.

The male frog is a dedicated daddy. After the female has laid her eggs, the male guards them. When the tadpoles hatch, they crawl onto the male's back and he carries them to water.

What's the difference between a poisonous and a venomous animal? A venomous creature, such as a snake, injects its toxin using fangs, spines, or stingers. A poisonous creature delivers its toxin passively, through being touched or eaten.

These frogs are endangered and live in a small area of Colombian rainforest, under threat from loggers and miners. But now there is a special nature reserve to protect them.

Lake
Maracaibo

VENEZUELA

The lightning begins inside dense,
towering storm clouds, which
can reach up to 7.5 miles high.

There can be
as many as
28 flashes in a
single minute.

Humid air above the lake rises, carrying water
droplets. These collide with ice crystals inside the clouds,
creating electric charges that zig-zag to the ground.

Many fishermen ply their trade on the waters
of Lake Maracaibo, but they make sure they are
safely back on shore by the time the lightning begins.

MARVEL AT THE
EVERLASTING LIGHTNING STORM, VENEZUELA

On most nights of the year something remarkable takes place in Venezuela, where the Catatumbo River flows into Lake Maracaibo. This place is home to a natural wonder unlike any other: a seemingly everlasting lightning storm. For up to nine or ten hours a night, on about 260 nights of the year, bolts of lightning illuminate the sky. They sometimes strike hundreds of times per hour. In fact, this area of Venezuela is the lightning capital of the world, with more strikes per square foot than anywhere else on Earth.

This dramatic light show has been taking place for as long as people can remember—possibly for thousands of years. So what causes this strange phenomenon? It's a bit of a mystery as to why this area alone produces such spectacular storms, night after night. However, experts think the lightning is triggered by warm air from the Caribbean Sea colliding with cold air flowing down from the Andes mountains. Whatever the cause, it makes for a thrilling show!

The most spectacular months for the lightning are October and November, at the height of the rainy season. The storms ease off in January and February, when the weather is dryer.

The storms can be seen from up to 250 miles away. In the past, sailors used the flashes of light to help them navigate... like a natural lighthouse!

This is the only place on Earth where lightning storms occur in the same place, night after night.

The lightning bolts can appear eerily quiet, without obvious thunder, but this is because they are often seen from a long way away.

Legend has it that the Catatumbo Lightning once saved the city of Maracaibo from invasion. One night in 1595, the English privateer Sir Francis Drake planned a surprise attack...

...But the lightning gave the game away, alerting the local soldiers to the position of Drake's ships.

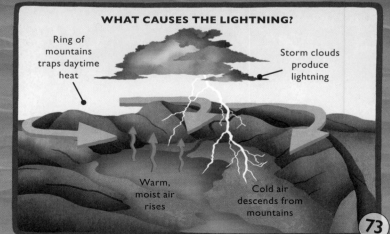

WHAT CAUSES THE LIGHTNING?

Ring of mountains traps daytime heat

Storm clouds produce lightning

Warm, moist air rises

Cold air descends from mountains

BRAZIL

Snake
Island

A golden lancehead uses special
heat detectors on its head to sense
its prey. Then it strikes, sinking its
fangs into its victim and injecting
a venom that kills instantly.

These vipers are bird-hunting
experts. The local birds are wise
to these dangerous predators,
but when migrating birds
stop by, the snakes get
ready to strike...

STEER CLEAR OF THE
DEADLIEST ISLAND ON EARTH, BRAZIL

The island spans less than half a square mile, but is home to between 2,000 and 4,000 golden lanceheads: the highest concentration of venomous snakes in the world.

These vipers measure about 27 inches. Their dappled, golden-brown scales help them hide among the island's foliage.

About 18 miles off the coast of Brazil is a tropical island which, from a distance, looks like paradise. But you'd be risking your life to set foot on it. This is the Ilha de Queimada Grande, also known as Snake Island. It is home to thousands of golden lancehead vipers, which are among the most venomous snakes in world. According to some, there's a snake for every square meter of land... so one wrong step could be fatal.

This deadly island has been closed to visitors since the 1920s. For the public's safety, and for the protection of the endangered snakes, nobody is allowed to disembark here without a special permit... along with a doctor and full medical supplies. The golden lancehead's venom is said to be five times stronger than the venom of their cousins on the mainland. One bite could melt your flesh and kill you in less than an hour. Luckily, the snakes can't swim!

How did the snakes come to be here? About 11,000 years ago there was a rise in sea levels, which cut the island off from the mainland...

...The snakes that were trapped here had no natural predators, so they quickly multiplied, evolving separately from their mainland cousins.

These snakes are unique: this species is not found in the wild anywhere else on Earth.

RECORD-BREAKING SNAKES

Most venomous snake: inland taipan, Australia

Heaviest snake: anaconda, South America

Longest snake: reticulated python, Asia

Fastest snake: black mamba, Africa

HEAR THE CALL OF THE WORLD'S
LOUDEST LAND ANIMAL, PERU

Each morning in the warm, humid jungles of Peru, a familiar sound can be heard echoing through the trees. This is the roar of the howler monkey. These creatures are famous for having one of the loudest calls in the animal kingdom. Their whooping howls can be heard over three miles away, even through dense rainforest. The calls can reach an ear-splitting volume of 90 decibels: as loud as a subway train!

The male howler monkeys are the noisy ones, calling far and wide at dawn and dusk to warn rival males to keep their distance. These territorial creatures use their deep, booming calls to defend their turf and guard their mates. 'I'M HERE!' they seem to say. 'Don't even try muscling in on my patch!' Fortunately for the neighbors, howler monkeys sleep for up to 15 hours a day, so peace and quiet returns to the jungle eventually.

These noisy creatures live in a family group, called a troop, of about ten monkeys.

The troop has to be on the lookout for harpy eagles. These deadly predators are sometimes strong enough to snatch adult monkeys, who can equal their own body weight!

The howler monkey is the loudest animal on land, but the blue whale is the loudest creature on Earth. Its 188-decibel call is louder than a jet plane taking off!

Baby howler monkeys stay with their mum until they are two. When male youngsters become adults, they move on to join a new troop.

Howler monkeys have amazing tails that loop around branches to act as an extra arm, or a safety rope. This kind of grasping tail is called a "prehensile tail."

Cup-shaped bone in throat amplifies the call

Long, prehensile tail for gripping branches

Strong, grasping toes

76

Red
howler
monkey
habitat

PERU

The monkeys have
an amazing sense of
smell: they can sniff out
tasty food from
over a mile away!

Why is the howler
monkey's call so loud?
A special cup-shaped bone
in the throat creates an echo
chamber that amplifies
the sound.

The males howl not only to mark
their territory, but also to impress
the ladies. Females are attracted to the
males with the deepest voices.

There are several species of howler monkey in Central
and South America. The red howler monkey lives
in the western Amazon Rainforest, in Colombia,
Venezuela, Ecuador, Peru and western Brazil.

The basin of the Amazon River contains the famous Amazon Rainforest: home to more than two million different species of plants and animals.

Keep your eyes peeled for the black caiman, one of the river's most deadly predators.

If you're lucky, you might spot a family of giant otters. They can grow over six feet long, making them the largest otters in the world.

The first person to paddle the entire length of the Amazon was the Polish kayaker Piotr Chmieliński, who completed the trip in 1986.

Kayaking some parts of the river can be dangerous, because of violent storms and waves. In some places, there are other threats, including modern-day pirates.

PERU

BRAZIL

River Amazon

Every year in the rainy season, the river bursts its banks and floods a vast area of forest. During the floods, some parts of the river reach over 30 miles wide!

In 2013 the American adventurer Darcy Gaechter became the first woman to kayak the Amazon from source to sea. It took her and her team 148 days.

Traveling around this area is difficult because of the thick jungle, so the mighty Amazon is the main transport route, with many boats carrying goods up and down.

One of the river's most famous residents is the pink river dolphin. These whiskered freshwater dolphins are almost blind, but they find their way around in the murky waters using sonar, like their ocean cousins.

There is no bridge crossing anywhere along the Amazon, so people use ferries to get from bank to bank.

PADDLE DOWN THE
BIGGEST RIVER IN THE WORLD, THE AMAZON

There's a hotly contested debate over which is the longest river in the world—the Nile, in Africa, or the Amazon, in South America. It's hard to measure a river's length: they often have several different sources, and some even have various end points, where they meet the sea. For many years, the Nile was believed to be the longest, but in 2007 Brazilian scientists used new satellite pictures to measure the Amazon, and concluded that it was 4,344 miles long: 217 miles longer than previously thought! If this is correct, it would mean the Amazon is longer than the Nile (which is thought to measure 4,258 kilometres).Whichever river scoops gold for length, the Amazon is definitely the biggest in terms of volume, carrying more water than the next seven largest rivers combined. In fact, it carries more than a fifth of all the fresh water on Earth! The Amazon and the streams that feed into it flow through six different countries: Peru, Ecuador, Colombia, Venezuela, Bolivia, and Brazil. These streams begin high in the steep Andes Mountains, gradually flattening out and merging into a vast channel that winds through the jungle until it meets the Atlantic Ocean. In places, the river is nearly ten miles wide, and even wider in the rainy season.

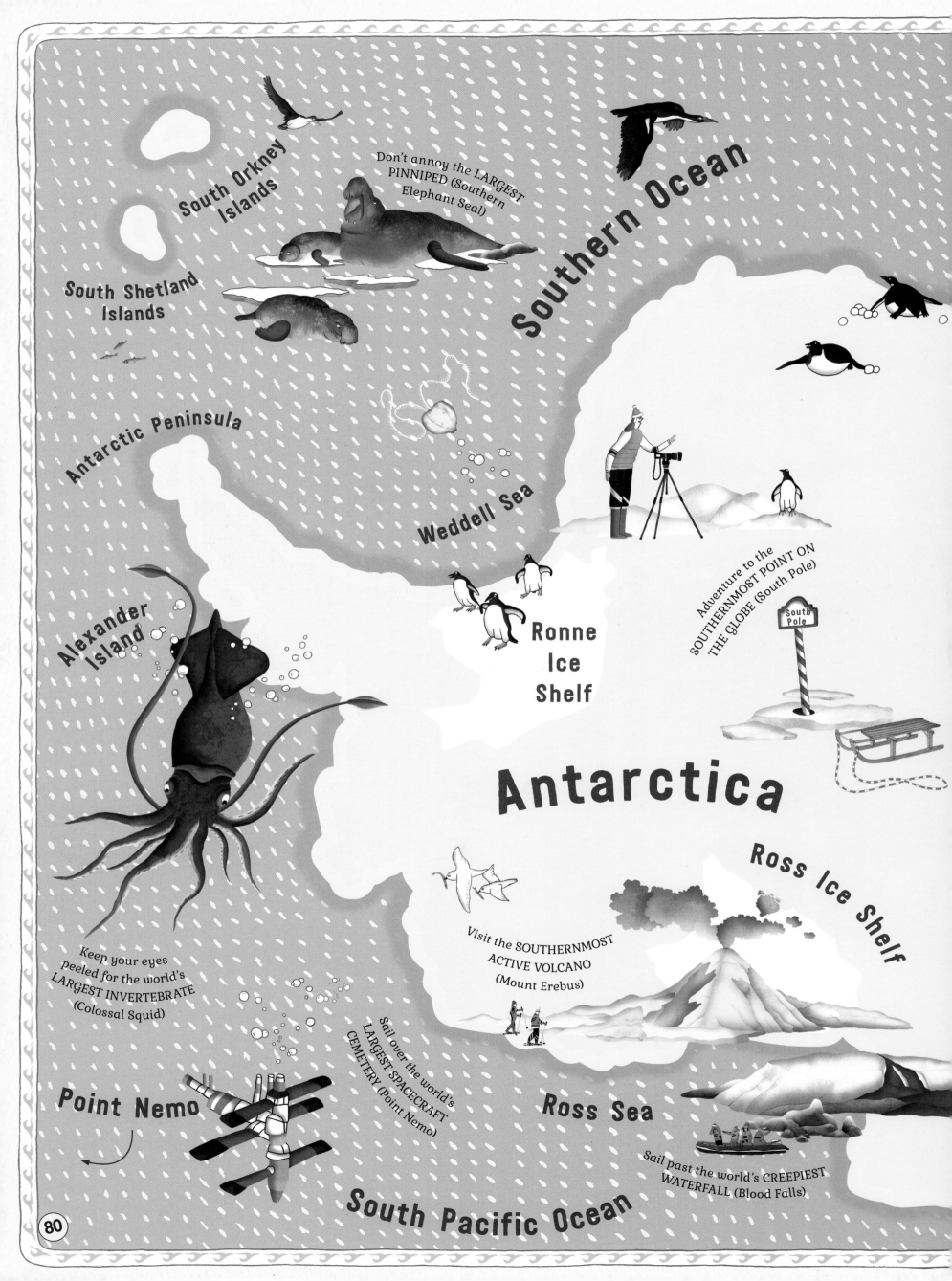

South Orkney Islands

Don't annoy the LARGEST PINNIPED (Southern Elephant Seal)

Southern Ocean

South Shetland Islands

Antarctic Peninsula

Weddell Sea

Adventure to the SOUTHERNMOST POINT ON THE GLOBE (South Pole)

South Pole

Alexander Island

Ronne Ice Shelf

Antarctica

Ross Ice Shelf

Keep your eyes peeled for the world's LARGEST INVERTEBRATE (Colossal Squid)

Visit the SOUTHERNMOST ACTIVE VOLCANO (Mount Erebus)

Sail over the world's LARGEST SPACECRAFT CEMETERY (Point Nemo)

Point Nemo

Ross Sea

Sail past the world's CREEPIEST WATERFALL (Blood Falls)

South Pacific Ocean

ANTARCTICA

Antarctica is a place of extremes. This ice-bound land mass at the bottom of the world breaks many records. As well as being the coldest continent on Earth, it is also the driest, and the windiest! At the turn of the 20th century, the goal of becoming the first person to reach the South Pole became a hotly contested prize among explorers. The Norwegian explorer Roald Amundsen won the race to the pole in 1911.

Huddle up with the LARGEST SPECIES OF PENGUIN (Emperor Penguin)

Amery Ice Shelf

Davis Sea

Indian Ocean

Shackleton Ice Shelf

Endure sub-zero temperatures at the COLDEST PLACE on Earth (Vostok Station)

Survive the WINDIEST PLACE on Earth (Commonwealth Bay)

ENDURE SUB-ZERO TEMPERATURES AT THE
COLDEST PLACE ON EARTH, ANTARCTICA

Welcome to the coldest neighborhood on the planet. This is the Vostok research station, which lies in the middle of the vast East Antarctic Ice Sheet. It's one of the most isolated, remote places in the world. In 1982, Russian scientists here recorded the lowest air temperature ever measured at a weather station: a bone-chilling -128.6°F. Then, in 2018, scientists used satellites to record even colder temperatures further up on the ice sheet, a few hundred miles away from Vostok. These broke more records, measuring an astounding -148°F: the lowest temperature ever recorded anywhere on Earth!

Living at the bottom of the world is hard. In summer, Vostok is home to about 25 scientists and engineers, but the number shrinks when the polar winter takes hold. Without the correct clothing, you would survive outside for only about three minutes. And it's not just the freezing temperatures that cause problems. Because Vostok lies at a high altitude, there's a low level of oxygen in the air, which can cause breathing difficulties. People here suffer from headaches, nosebleeds, ear pains, and high blood pressure, as well as frostbite!

Where are the penguins? Here at the "Pole of Cold," as it is called, it's too chilly even for them, and too far away from the sea. They live elsewhere in Antarctica.

CANBERRA 5,182 KM

MOSCOW 15,575 KM

WELLINGTON 5,053 KM   CAPE TOWN 6,282 KM

NEW DELHI 12,053 KM

LONDON 15,710 KM   NEW YORK 14,509 KM

PARIS 15,446 KM

BEIJING 13,169 KM

The average winter temperature in Antarctica is about -52°C. That's cold, especially when you consider that your freezer at home is only about -0.4°C!

When it's really cold, researchers have to breathe through special masks, which warm up the freezing air before it is inhaled.

Scientists are carried to and from the research station via plane.

In the Antarctic winter, between late-April and mid-August, there is a "polar night" lasting about 120 days, when the sun never rises.

The Vostok station is the most isolated of all the Antarctic research bases. It lies more than 621 miles from the coast, at 11,443 feet above sea level.

ANTARCTICA

Vostok Station

Research scientists drill into the ice to study the history of Antarctica's climate.

In the 1990s scientists discovered that over 13,000 feet below the ice, beneath Vostok Station, is an enormous freshwater lake. Lake Vostok is about the same size as North America's Lake Ontario.

Lake Vostok has been sealed off by ice for about 15 million years, but despite lying under the coldest spot on the planet, it's not frozen! Geothermal heat from inside the Earth stops it from getting too cold.

A BURIED LAKE

Vostok Station

Ice sheet

Frozen water

Lake Vostok

Liquid water

CAN YOU FIND?

 A cheetah cub with a stopwatch, **Botswana**

 A candle, **New Zealand**

 A caiman in a pirate hat, **The Amazon**

 A lamp shade, **USA**

 A bonnet, **Canada**

 A gorilla yawning, **Rwanda**

 A ladder, **USA**

 A basket of fruit, **Turkey**

 Ketchup and mustard, **USA**

 A stone letter "M", **France**

 A snow plow, **Antarctica**

 A toucan, **Peru**

 A marathon-running dog, **Morocco**

 A zebra having a drink, **Botswana**

 A gazelle mopping its brow, **Botswana**

 A decorated storage pot, **Turkey**

 A marmot with a checkered flag, **Mongolia**

 A clothespin on a bird's beak, **Indonesia**

 A flying marlin, **Australia**

 A branch in a vase, **New Zealand**

 An acrobatic gibbon, **Indonesia**

 A shovel, **Mongolia**

 A camel with a green rug, **Ethiopia**

 A parakeet with a pretzel, **USA**

 A black and yellow warning sign, **The Bahamas**

 A frog carrying tadpoles, **Colombia**

 A bear rowing a boat, **Canada**

 Someone in a pink bathing suit, **Zambia**

 A wheelbarrow of snow, **Antarctica**

 A megaphone, **USA**

Swimming goggles, **The Azores**

A purple pot plant, **Venezuela**

A coconut drink, **The Bahamas**

A hawk with a holdall, **Canada**

A clam, **Greenland**

A mail box, **Mongolia**

A prairie dog portrait, **USA**

A fish being skewered, **Australia**

A slice of cake, **Greenland**

A lobster pot, **The Azores**

Someone reading a map, **Vietnam**

A bucket and spade, **Antarctica**

A church, **Greenland**

A sleeping baby monkey, **Peru**

A waving Baikal sea, **Russia**

A bird with a fish, **Russia**

A monocle, **Greenland**

A donkey in sunglasses, **Turkey**

A basket of berries, **New Zealand**

A waving kangaroo, **Australia**

A crown made of leaves, **Rwanda**

A peregrine with a Lady Liberty hat, **USA**

A straw hat, **The Bahamas**

A monkey with binoculars, **Peru**

A rocking chair, **USA**

A frill-necked lizard, **Australia**

A boat's periscope, **Italy**

A spotted handkerchief, **Brazil**

85

INDEX

Atlas of Record-Breaking Adventures © copyright Wide Eyed Editions 2020
Illustrations © copyright Lucy Letherland 2020
Text © copyright Emily Hawkins 2020

First Published in 2020 by Wide Eyed Editions, an imprint of The Quarto Group.
100 Cummings Center, Suite 265D, Beverly, MA 01915, USA.
T +1 978-282-9590 F +1 978-283-2742 **www.QuartoKnows.com**

ISBN 978-0-7112-5565-4

Illustrated with colored inks
Set in Festivo, Gabriela and Gill Sans Shadow

Designed by Myrto Dimitrakoulia
Edited by Lucy Brownridge
Published by Georgia Amson-Bradshaw
Production by Dawn Cameron

Printed in Malaysia VV072020

1 3 5 7 9 8 6 4 2

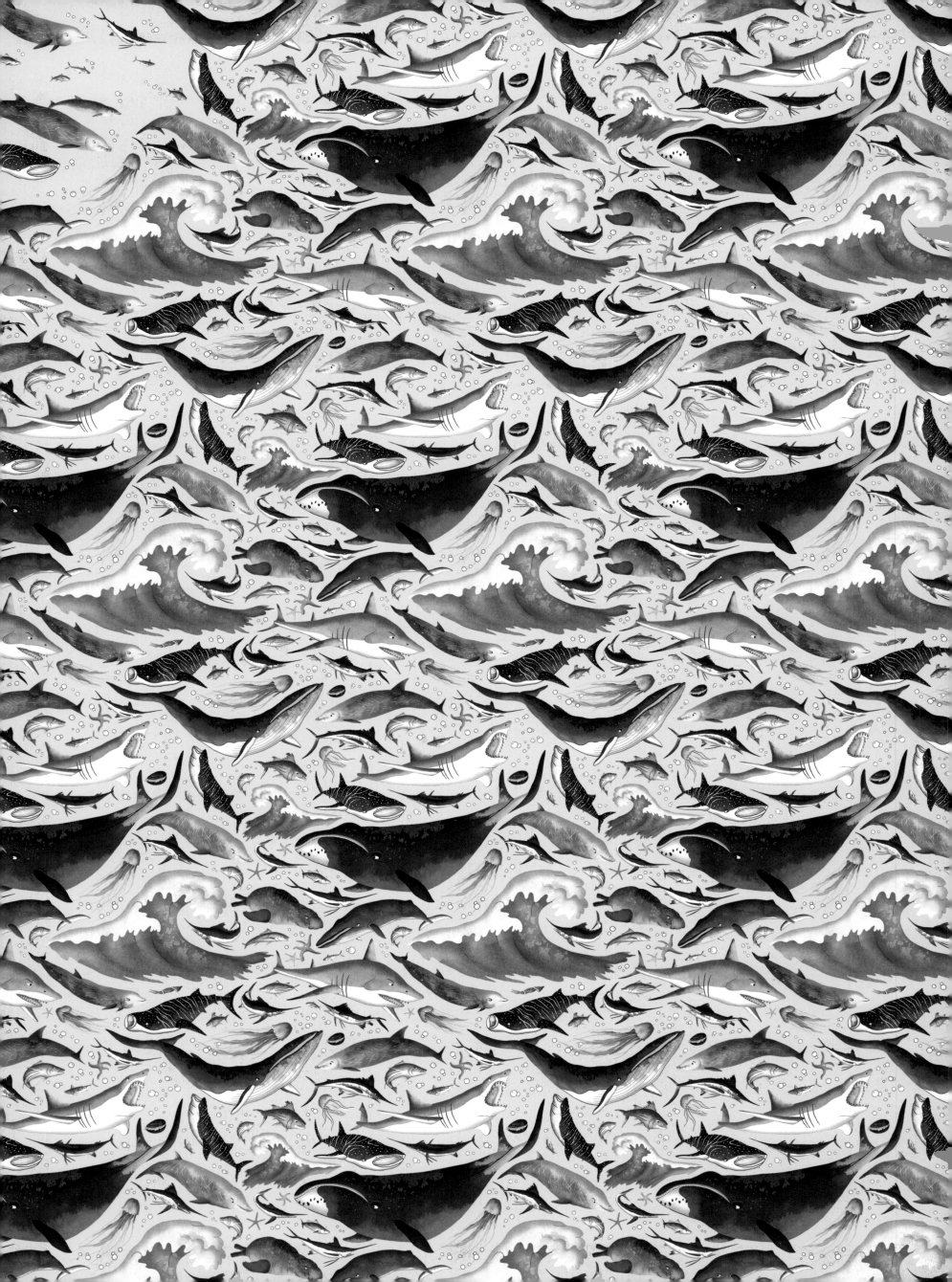